THE OBSERVER'S
POCKET   SERIES
.   .   .

THE OBSERVER'S BOOK OF RAILWAY LOCOMOTIVES OF BRITAIN

The Observer's Books

THE OBSERVER'S BOOK OF

RAILWAY
LOCOMOTIVES
OF BRITAIN

Revised and Edited

by

H. C. CASSERLEY

*Describing the steam locomotives of Britain,
with 8 colour plates and over 200 photo-
graphs. Also including a list of diesel and
electric locomotives in general use.*

FREDERICK WARNE & CO. LTD.
LONDON
FREDERICK WARNE & CO. INC.
NEW YORK

CONTENTS

5

PREFACE

THIS little volume is primarily intended as a pocket-book to enable the observer to recognise the majority of locomotives he sees in his wanderings through either familiar or unfamiliar territory, showing him at a glance their histories, specifications and performances.

The essential descriptions given will be found more than sufficient to enable an engine to be recognised easily without excessive technical skill or engineering knowledge, providing the book is used correctly. To this end it is recommended that the method of use outlined on pages 24 to 26 is followed as closely as possible. The greater part of the book is devoted to steam locomotives, as they have a far greater general appeal than the more soulless electrics and diesels which are destined gradually to replace them. As the numbers of the latter increase, it may be necessary in future editions to give more space to their description, but so long as the well-loved steam locomotives still remain with us in considerable number the major part of this book will be devoted to them.

The writer desires to express to the Public Relations Officers of the various Regions of British Railways and the British Transport Commission his thanks for their kind co-operation and their permission to use some official pictures of the locomotives illustrated in these pages. Particulars have been brought up to date, as far as possible, to approximately Midsummer 1960, and in this new edition details of the steam and electric locomotives owned by the London Transport Board have also been included for the first time.

INTRODUCTION

IT will be noted that a considerable rearrangement in the order of presentation of the various classes has been effected in this revised edition of *The Observer's Book of Locomotives*. In former editions the engines were grouped as far as possible into the Regional divisional system adopted by British Railways in 1948. This, however, was by no means an ideal system, even in the earlier stages when the newly formed Regions roughly corresponded to the lines of the former four main groups, for six Regions were formed out of four railways, the L.N.E.R. being divided amongst two newly formed Regions, the Eastern and the North Eastern, whilst the Scottish Region was composed partly of former L.M.S. and L.N.E.R. lines.

Since then, however, there have been numerous readjustments to the Regional boundaries with little regard to the operational standpoint, with the result that in many cases through main and branch lines are now chopped up between the different arbitrary Regional boundaries, and this process is still going on, consequently any attempt to classify any particular class of locomotive as belonging to a particular Region is largely meaningless. For example, the well-known class 5 mixed traffic locomotives of the former L.M.S.R. are now to be found stationed in and operating over lines of all the six Regions. This applies also to the various standard designs which have been introduced since 1948, none of which—with the possible exception of the "Clan" class 4-6-0's and the solitary "Duke of Gloucester"—can be regarded as belonging to any particular Region.

It is felt, therefore, that a far simpler and more logical method of presentation is to be had by arranging the classes as far as possible in numerical order. This results automatically in bringing together all the locomotives of each of the four groups: for all were renumbered in block in 1948, the Great Western engines retaining their old numbers which were all below 10000, the Southern in the 30000's, the L.M.S. in the 40000's and 50000's and the L.N.E.R. in the 60000's. The numbers 70000 upwards were allocated to new designs, whilst the 10000's were reserved for Diesel locomotives and the 20000's for electric engines. Recently, however, a new system has been adopted with regard to the Diesels, under which, with one or two exceptions, they are numbered in a separate series with the prefix "D".

It should be remembered that consecutive numbers do not always mean that the engines concerned are of the same type.

In each locomotive type a general idea of the locality in which it is likely to be seen is added, so that a double check is provided; but nowadays it is not unusual for engines to be found many hundreds of miles from their ancestral home, working on a strange Region.

The list of locomotive superintendents and motive power engineers responsible for the design and building of the many different types of British Railways locomotives, together with the dates during which they held office, is given on pages 12 and 13. A table showing the original pre-grouping (pre-1923) companies which formed the "Big Four" (London Midland and Scottish, London and North Eastern, Southern and Great Western Railways) is given on pages 10 and 11. It was these four major companies which were finally amalgamated to form British Railways in 1948, when the grouped companies lost their identities.

CONSTITUTION OF THE
FOUR PRE-GROUPING RAILWAY
COMPANIES

GREAT WESTERN RAILWAY

Great Western Railway
Barry Railway (1 Jan. 1922)
Cambrian Railways (1 Jan. 1922)
Cardiff Railway (1 Jan. 1922)
Rhymney Railway (1 Jan. 1922)
Taff Vale Railway (1 Jan. 1922)
Alexandra (Newport and South Wales) Docks and Railway (1 Jan. 1922)
Brecon and Merthyr Railway (1 July 1922)
Vale of Rheidol Railway (1 Jan. 1922)*
Burry Port and Gwendraeth Valley Railway (1 July 1922)
Cleobury Mortimer and Ditton Priors Light Railway (1 Jan. 1922)
Llanelly and Mynydd Mawr Railway (1923)
Weston, Clevedon and Portishead Railway (1940)
Welshpool and Llanfair Light Railway (1 Jan. 1922)*
Swansea Harbour Trust Railways (1923)
Neath and Brecon Railway (1 July 1922)
Gwendraeth Valleys Railway (1923)
Midland and South Western Junction Railway (1923)
Powlesland and Mason, Swansea Docks (1 Jan. 1924)
Corris Railway (4 Aug. 1930)
Port Talbot Railway and Docks Co.†
Rhondda and Swansea Bay Railway†
South Wales Mineral Railway†

* Previously absorbed by Cambrian Railways.
† Absorbed in 1907, but independently worked until 1922.

LONDON, MIDLAND AND SCOTTISH RAILWAY

Caledonian Railway
Furness Railway
Glasgow and South Western Railway
Highland Railway
Lancashire and Yorkshire Railway*
London and North Western Railway
London, Tilbury and Southend Railway†
Maryport and Carlisle Railway

* Renamed London and North Western Railway (Division B) in Jan. 1922, on absorption into the L. & N.W.R. (which then became Division A).
† Absorbed by Midland Railway in 1912.

Midland Railway
Somerset and Dorset Joint Railway*
Cleator and Workington Junction Railway
Glasgow and Paisley Joint Line
Knott End Railway
Leek and Manifold Light Railway†
Stratford-on-Avon and Midland Junction Railway
North Staffordshire Railway
Wirral Railway
North London Railway‡

  * Worked jointly with Southern Railway.
  † Worked by North Staffordshire Railway.
  ‡ Worked by L.N.W.R. from Dec. 1908.

LONDON AND NORTH EASTERN RAILWAY

Great Northern Railway (including the East and West Yorkshire Union Railway)
North Eastern Railway
Great Eastern Railway (including Colne Valley and Halstead Railway, 1 July 1923, Mid Suffolk Light Railway, 1 July 1924)
Great Central Railway
Hull and Barnsley Railway*
North British Railway
Great North of Scotland Railway
Manchester, Sheffield and Lincolnshire Railway†
Midland and Great Northern Joint Railway‡
Metropolitan Railway—18 locos. taken over Nov. 1937 (rest to London Transport)

  * Taken over by the North Eastern Railway on 1 April 1922.
  † Renamed Great Central Railway in 1897.
  ‡ Worked jointly with London, Midland and Scottish Railway until 1 Oct. 1936.

SOUTHERN RAILWAY

London and South Western Railway (including the Plymouth, Devonport and South Western Junction Railway)
London, Brighton and South Coast Railway
South Eastern and Chatham Railway*
Lynton and Barnstaple Railway (1 July 1923)
Freshwater, Yarmouth and Newport Railway
Isle of Wight Railway
Isle of Wight Central Railway

  * Previously to 1899, the two companies composing the S.E. & C.R. were the South Eastern Railway and the London, Chatham and Dover Railway. They formed a joint working committee in that year under the new title.

BRITISH LOCOMOTIVE
SUPERINTENDENTS AND
CHIEF MECHANICAL ENGINEERS

Adams, W.	L.S.W.R.	1878–1895
Archbutt, R. C.	S. & D.J.R.	1913–1930
Aspinall, John A. F.	L. & Y.R.	1886–1899
Barton Wright, W.	L. & Y.R.	1876–1886
Beattie, J. H.	L. & S.W.R.	1850–1871
Beattie, W. G.	L. & S.W.R.	1871–1878
Billinton, Lawson, B.	L.B. & S.C.	1911–1922
Billinton, R. J.	L.B. & S.C.	1890–1904
Bowen-Cooke, Charles J.	L.N.W.R.	1909–1920
Bulleid, O. V.	S.R.	1937–1947
Chalmers, W.	N.B.R.	1919–1922
Churchward, G. J.	G.W.R.	1902–1921
Collett, Charles B.	G.W.R.	1921–1941
Cumming, C.	Highland Ry.	1915–1923
Dean, William	G.W.R.	1877–1902
Deeley, R. M.	Midland Ry.	1903–1909
Drummond, Dugald	Cal. R.	1882–1890
	L. & S.W.R.	1895–1912
Drummond, Peter	Highland Ry.	1896–1911
Dunbar, J.	Brecon and Merthyr Ry.	1917–1923
Fairburn, C. E.	L.M.S.	1944–1945
Fowler, Sir Henry	Midland Ry.	1909–1923
	L.M.S.	1925–1931
Gresley, Sir Nigel	Great Northern	1911–1922
	L.N.E.R.	1923–1941
Hawksworth, F. W.	G.W.R.	1941–1948
Heywood, T. E.	G.N. of S.	1914–1922
Hill, A. J.	G.E.R.	1912–1922
Holden, J.	G.E.R.	1885–1907
Holden, S. D.	G.E.R.	1908–1912
Holmes, M.	Nth. British	1882–1903
Hughes, George	L. & Y.R.	1904–1921
	L.N.W.R.	1921–1922
	L.M.S.	1923–1925
Hurry-Riches, I.	Taff Vale Ry.	1873–1911

Ivatt, H. A.	G.N.R.	1896–1911
Ivatt, H. G.	L.M.S.	1945–1947
Johnson, J.	G.N. of S.	1890–1894
Johnson, S. W.	G.E.R.	1866–1873
	Midland Ry.	1873–1903
Kirtley, W.	L.C. & D.R.	1874–1898
Marsh, D. Earle	L.B. & S.C.	1905–1911
Maunsell, R. E. L.	S.E. & C.R.	1913–1922
	S.R.	1923–1937
McIntosh, J.	Caledonian Ry.	1895–1914
Park, J. C.	Nth. London	1873–1893
Parker, T.	M.S. & L.	1886–1893
Peppercorn, A. H.	L.N.E.R.	1946–1949
Pettigrew, W. F.	Furness Ry.	1897–1918
Pickersgill, W.	G.N. of S.	1894–1914
	Caledonian Ry.	1914–1923
Pollitt, H.	M. S. & L.	1893–1897
	G.C.R.	1898–1900
Raven, Sir Vincent	N.E.R.	1910–1922
Reid, W. P.	N.B.R.	1903–1919
Riddles, R. A., C.B.E.	British Rlys.	1948–1953
Robinson, J. G.	G.C.R.	1900–1922
Stanier, Sir William	L.M.S.	1932–1944
Stirling, J.	South Eastern	1878–1898
Stirling, Patrick	G.N.R.	1866–1895
Stroudley, William	L.B. & S.C.	1870–1889
Thompson, E.	L.N.E.R.	1941–1946
Urie, R. W.	L.S.W.R.	1912–1922
Wainwright, H.	S.E. & C.R.	1899–1913
Webb, Francis William	L.N.W.R.	1871–1903
Whitelegg, R. H.	L.T. & S.R.	1910–1912
	G. & S.W.R.	1918–1923
Whitelegg, Thomas	L.T. & S.R.	1880–1910
Worsdell, T. W.	N.E.R.	1885–1890
Worsdell, Wilson	N.E.R.	1890–1910

STANDARD LOCOMOTIVE
HEADLAMP CODE

1. Express Passenger Train. Breakdown Train going to clear the line, or Light Engine going to assist disabled train. Empty Coaching-Stock Train timed at express passenger train speed.

2. Ordinary Passenger Train. Mixed Train. Breakdown Train not going to clear the line. Branch Passenger Train. Rail Motor Train or Railcar.

3. Express Freight or Ballast Train authorised to run at a maximum speed of 35 m.p.h. Empty Coaching-Stock Train not carrying headlamps for group "1".

4. Parcels, Newspaper, Fish, Meat, Fruit, Milk, Horse-box, Cattle or Perishable Goods Train composed of vacuum-braked stock with brake-pipe connected to engine. Express Freight Train. Livestock, Perishable or Ballast Train with not less than one-third of the vacuum-braked vehicles connected to the engine.

5. Freight, Mineral or Ballast Train. Train of empties carrying a through load to destination.

6. Express Freight, Fish, Meat, Fruit or Cattle Train. Ballast Train not running under group "3" or "4" headlamps. Special Train conveying 36-ton breakdown crane but not proceeding to an accident.

7. Through Fast Train not running under group "3", "4", or "5" headlamps and carrying a through load.

8. Light Engine or Light Engines coupled together. Engine and brake-van.

9. Freight, Mineral, or Ballast Train stopping at intermediate stations.

10. Ballast, Freight, or Inspection Train requiring to stop in between signal boxes (in the section). Branch Freight Train.

N.B. Headlamp codes are subject to alteration in the case of "through" trains working over branch lines, and also to minor variations on the different Regions of British Railways.

*BRITISH RAILWAYS LIVERIES

STANDARD engine liveries have been adopted for use on British Railways as follows:

† Express Passenger classes.   Dark green, lined out in black and orange.

Other Passenger and Mixed Traffic classes.   Black, lined out in red, cream and grey.

Freight and Shunting classes.   Black, unlined.

* See coloured diagrams.
† Many former Great Western engines of other than express passenger classes, including small passenger tank engines, are now being repainted at Swindon in the lined-out dark green, which is the former G.W.R. standard colour.
Some of the L.M.S. Pacifics are painted in maroon; lined out with black and yellow, the former livery of L.M.S.R. express types, which was in turn inherited (with a slightly darker shade of red) from the old Midland Railway.
The restored engines detailed on pages 28–32 and 49 are painted in their respective pre-grouping colour. Diesel and electric locomotives are normally given the G.W.R. green similar to the express steam classes, although there have been one or two experimental liveries applied here and there.
Some of the "J–72" class o–6–oT's, such as 68736 used on station pilot work at York, Darlington and Newcastle, have been painted in the light green of the former North Eastern Railway and "J–69" class o–6–oT No. 68619, on similar duties at Liverpool Street, has likewise been turned out in dark blue after the style of the old Great Eastern Railway.
London Transport engines, both steam and electric, (pages 237–242) are painted in a dark shade of red, lined out in black and yellow.

LIST OF COLOUR PLATES

Plate 1. Stanier Pacific No. 46210 "Lady Patricia" on Liverpool Express

Plate 2.   "King" Class No. 6000, "King George V"

Plate 3. British Railways Class 7-MT, No. 70009, "Alfred the Great"

Plate 4. Class 7-F 0–8–0 No. 49314 (L.N.W.R. Class G–2a)

Plate 5. *One hundred and twenty years of Evolution. West Country Class, "Yeovil" No. 34004, with Stephenson's "Rocket" in foreground*

Plate 6. *British Railways 2–6–4T Class 4–PT/4–FT No.* 80031

Plate 7. Gresley Class A-4 Pacific No. 60033, "Seagull"

1. Chimney
2. Top Feed Pipes
3. Dome
4. Safety-valves
5. Whistle
6. Firebox

7. Cab Look-outs
8. Cab Door
9. Bunker Side
10. Side Tank
11. Footplate
12. Driving Wheels

13. Crosshead
14. Cylinders
15. Sandbox
16. Front Buffer Beam
17. Brake-pipe Hose
18. Smokebox

Plate 8. Points to Look for when Identifying Locomotives

"WHYTE" WHEEL ARRANGEMENT

Wheel arrangement	Notation	Name of type
FRONT REAR		

	Notation	Name of type
	0–4–0	
	0–4–2	
	0–4–4	
	2–4–0	
	2–4–2	
	4–4–0	
	4–4–2	"Atlantic"
	0–6–0	
	0–6–2	
	2–6–0	"Mogul"
	2–6–2	"Prairie"
	2–6–4	
	4–6–0	
	4–6–2	"Pacific"
	0–8–0	
	2–8–0	"Consolidation"
	2–8–2	"Mikado"
	2–6–6–2	"Garratt"
	0–10–0	"Decapod"

BRITISH RAILWAYS SHED CODE

THE engine's running number is carried normally on the cabside of the locomotive (in the case of a few tank engines it appears on the tank side instead), and with very few exceptions also on the front of the engine on a rectangular plate affixed to the smokebox door. Beneath the latter will also be found a small oval plate bearing a number and letter which indicate the locomotive depot to which the engine belongs. The practice, both as regards the number plate on the smokebox door and the shed plate, can be traced back to the old Midland Railway, on which line it was adopted in pre-grouping days. This is not the only distinction inherited from the Midland to survive to the present time, for the livery of the coaching stock, dark red with yellow and black lining (also now being applied to some London Midland engines) is substantially the same as that adopted by the old M.R. for both locomotives and coaching stock in pre-grouping days.

It is often of considerable interest to know the home depot from which an engine is working, and the code is therefore tabulated in full on the following pages. The numbers are grouped according to Region, the main sheds in each case being followed by the letter A. The sub-depots bearing the suffixes B, C, D, etc., although nominally subsidiary to the A shed, are often sheds as large or larger than the parent one. Very small sheds, housing one or two or perhaps a few engines only, are not usually given separate code letters. They are shown in this list following the main shed, to which they are subsidiary. Thus, Stratford, whose code number is 30A (and which incidentally has the largest allocation of locomotives in the country) supplies engines for the smaller depots at Enfield Town, Wood Street, and so on.

Nowadays main line engines often work much

longer distances from their home depots than formerly, on intensive and complicated "rosters", under which an engine may be away from its home shed for several days and cover many parts of the system a long way from its depot. In many instances the newly created artificial geographical "Regions", of which further adjustments are continually being made, bear progressively less and less relation to the actual operational lines which must follow the main routes of the old Companies in such an organisation as railway transport. This of course results in many engines being found working over lines in Regions other than that to which they are attached; this is one of the reasons why it is no longer possible nor logical to describe any particular engine or class of engine as belonging to any specified Region.

BRITISH RAILWAYS LOCOMOTIVE SHEDS AND SHED CODES

All B.R. Locomotives carry the code of their home depot on a small plate affixed to the smokebox door.

LONDON MIDLAND
REGION

1A	Willesden
1B	Camden
1C	Watford
1D	Devons Road (Bow)
1E	Bletchley, Leighton Buzzard
2A	Rugby, Coventry
2B	Nuneaton
2E	Northampton
2F	Woodford Halse
5A	Crewe North, Whitchurch
5B	Crewe South
5C	Stafford
5D	Stoke
5E	Alsager
5F	Uttoxeter
6A	Chester (former L.N.W.R. shed)
6B	Mold Junction
6C	Birkenhead
6E	Chester (former G.W.R. shed)
6F	Bidston
6G	Llandudno Junction
6H	Bangor
6J	Holyhead
6K	Rhyl
8A	Edge Hill
8B	Warrington, Warrington (Arpley)
8C	Speke Junction

8D	Widnes
8E	Northwich
8F	Springs Branch (Wigan
8G	Sutton Oak
9A	Longsight (Manchester)
9B	Stockport (Edgeley)
9C	Macclesfield
9D	Buxton
9E	Trafford Park
9F	Heaton Mersey
9G	Gorton
12A	Carlisle (Kingmoor)
12B	Carlisle (Upperby), Penrith
12C	Carlisle (Canal)
12D	Kirkby Stephen
12E	Barrow
12F	Workington
12G	Oxenholme
12H	Tebay
14A	Cricklewood
14B	Kentish Town
14D	Neasden, Aylesbury, Chesham
14E	Bedford
15A	Wellingborough
15B	Kettering
15C	Leicester (former M.R. shed)
15D	Coalville
15E	Leicester (former G.C.R. shed)

15F	Market Harborough, Seaton	**EASTERN REGION**	
		30A	Stratford, Chelmsford, Enfield Town, Ilford, Wood Street (Walthamstow), Bishop's Stortford, Southend (Victoria)
16A	Nottingham		
16B	Kirkby		
16C	Mansfield		
16D	Annesley	30E	Colchester, Braintree, Maldon, Clacton, Walton
17A	Derby		
17B	Burton, Horninglow, Overseal	30F	Parkeston
17C	Rowsley, Cromford, Middleton, Sheep Pasture	31A	Cambridge, Ely
		31B	March
		31C	King's Lynn
18A	Toton		
18B	Westhouses		
18C	Hasland	32A	Norwich, Cromer Beach
		32B	Ipswich
21A	Saltley	32C	Lowestoft
21B	Bescot	32D	Yarmouth (South Town)
21C	Bushbury		
21D	Aston	33B	Tilbury
21E	Monument Lane	33C	Shoeburyness
21F	Walsall		
		34A	King's Cross
24A	Accrington	34B	Hornsey
24B	Rose Grove	34C	Hatfield
24C	Lostock Hall	34D	Hitchin
24D	Lower Darwen	34E	New England
24E	Blackpool, Blackpool North	34F	Grantham
24F	Fleetwood		
24G	Skipton	36A	Doncaster
24H	Hellifield	36C	Frodingham
24J	Lancaster	36E	Retford, Newark
24K	Preston		
24L	Carnforth	40A	Lincoln
		40B	Immingham, Grimsby, New Holland
26A	Newton Heath	40E	Colwick
26B	Agecroft	40F	Boston, Sleaford
26C	Bolton		
26D	Bury	41A	Sheffield (Darnall)
26E	Lees	41B	Sheffield (Grimesthorpe)
26F	Patricroft	41C	Millhouses
		41D	Canklow
27A	Bank Hall	41E	Staveley (former M.R. shed)
27B	Aintree	41F	Mexborough
27C	Southport	41H	Staveley (former G.C.R. shed)
27D	Wigan (L and Y)		
27E	Walton	41J	Langwith
27F	Brunswick		

NORTH EASTERN REGION

50A	York
50B	Hull (Dairycoates)
50C	Hull (Botanic Gardens)
50D	Goole
50E	Scarborough
50F	Malton

51A	Darlington
51C	West Hartlepool
51F	West Auckland
51J	Northallerton
51L	Thornaby

52A	Gateshead, Bowes Bridge
52B	Heaton
52C	Blaydon
52D	Tweedmouth, Alnmouth
52E	Percy Main
52F	North Blyth, South Blyth
52G	Sunderland, Durham
52H	Tyne Dock, Pelton Level
52K	Consett

55A	Leeds (Holbeck)
55B	Stourton
55C	Farnley Junction
55D	Royston
55E	Normanton
55F	Manningham
55G	Huddersfield
55H	Leeds (Neville Hill)

56A	Wakefield
56B	Ardsley
56C	Copley Hill
56D	Mirfield
56E	Sowerby Bridge
56F	Low Moor
56G	Bradford

SCOTTISH REGION

60A	Inverness, Dingwall, Kyle of Lochalsh
60B	Aviemore, Boat of Garten
60C	Helmsdale, Tain
60D	Wick, Thurso

61A	Kittybrewster (Aberdeen), Ballater, Fraserburgh, Inverurie, Peterhead
61B	Aberdeen (Ferryhill)
61C	Keith, Banff, Elgin

62A	Thornton, Anstruther, Burntisland, Ladybank, Methil
62B	Dundee (Tay Bridge), Arbroath, Montrose, St. Andrews
62C	Dunfermline, Alloa

63A	Perth, Aberfeldy, Blair Atholl, Forfar, Crieff
63B	Fort William, Mallaig
63C	Oban, Ballachulish

64A	St. Margaret's (Edinburgh), Dunbar, Galashiels, Longniddry, North Berwick, Seafield, South Leith
64B	Haymarket (Edinburgh)
64C	Dalry Road (Edinburgh)
64F	Bathgate
64G	Hawick
64H	Leith Central

65A	Eastfield (Glasgow) Arrochar
65B	St. Rollox
65C	Parkhead
65D	Dawsholm, Dumbarton
65E	Kipps
65F	Grangemouth
65G	Yoker
65H	Helensburgh
65I	Balloch
65J	Stirling
65K	Polmont

66A	Polmadie (Glasgow)	73E	Faversham
66B	Motherwell	73F	Ashford, Ramsgate
66C	Hamilton	73H	Dover, Folkestone
66D	Greenock (Ladyburn)	73J	Tonbridge
66E	Carstairs		

67A	Corkerhill (Glasgow)	75A	Brighton
67B	Hurlford, Beith, Muirkirk	75B	Redhill
		75C	Norwood Junction
		75E	Three Bridges, Horsham
67C	Ayr		
67D	Ardrossan	75F	Tunbridge Wells West

68B	Dumfries
68C	Stranraer, Newton Stewart
68D	Beattock

SOUTHERN REGION

70A	Nine Elms
70B	Feltham
70C	Guildford
70D	Basingstoke
70H	Ryde (I.O.W.)

71A	Eastleigh, Andover Junction, Lymington, Winchester
71B	Bournemouth, Branksome
71G	Weymouth, Bridport
71I	Southampton Docks

72A	Exmouth Junction, Bude, Exmouth, Lyme Regis, Okehampton, Seaton, Callington
72B	Salisbury
72C	Yeovil
72E	Barnstaple Junction, Ilfracombe, Torrington
72F	Wadebridge

73A	Stewarts Lane
73B	Bricklayers Arms
73C	Hither Green

WESTERN REGION

81A	Old Oak Common
81B	Slough, Marlow
81C	Southall
81D	Reading
81E	Didcot
81F	Oxford, Fairford

82A	Bristol (Bath Rd.), Bath, Wells, Weston-super-Mare, Yatton
82B	St. Philip's Marsh (Bristol)
82C	Swindon, Chippenham
82D	Westbury, Frome
82E	Bristol (former M.R. shed)
82F	Bath (S & D), Radstock, Highbridge
82G	Templecombe

83A	Newton Abbot, Kingsbridge
83B	Taunton, Bridgwater
83C	Exeter, Tiverton Junction
83D	Laira (Plymouth), Launceston
83E	St. Blazey, Bodmin Moorswater
83F	Truro
83G	Penzance, Helston, St. Ives
83H	Plymouth Friary

84A	Wolverhampton (Stafford Rd.)	87D	Swansea East Dock, Upper Bank
84B	Oxley	87E	Landore
84C	Banbury	87F	Llanelly, Burry Port, Pantyfynnon, Llandovery
84D	Leamington Spa		
84E	Tyseley, Stratford-on-Avon		
84F	Stourbridge Junction	87G	Carmarthen, Abercynon
84G	Kidderminster		
84H	Wellington (Salop)	87H	Neyland, Cardigan, Milford Haven, Pembroke Dock, Whitland
		87J	Goodwick (Fishguard)
85A	Worcester, Evesham, Kingham		
		88A	Cardiff (Canton), Radyr
85B	Gloucester (G.W.R.), Brimscombe, Cheltenham, Lydney, Ross-on-Wye	88B	
		88C	Barry
		88D	Methyr, Cae Harris, Dowlais Central, Rhymney
85C	Gloucester, (M.R.), Dursley, Tewkesbury		
		88E	Abercynon
85D	Bromsgrove, Redditch	88F	Treherbert, Ferndale
		88G	Llantrisant
		88H	Tondu
		88J	Aberdare
		88K	Brecon
86A	Newport (Ebbw Junction)		
		89A	Shrewsbury, Builth Rd., Craven Arms, Knighton, Leominster
86B	Newport (Pill)		
86C	Hereford		
86E	Severn Tunnel Junction		
86F	Aberbeeg	89B	Croes Newydd, Bala, Penmaenpool, Trawsfynydd
86G	Pontypool Road		
		89C	Machynlleth, Aberystwyth, Aberystwyth (V of R), Portmadoc, Pwllheli
87A	Neath, Glyn Neath, Neath (N & B)		
87B	Duffryn Yard	89D	Oswestry, Llandiloes, Moat Lane
87C	Danygraig		

METHOD OF IDENTIFYING A LOCOMOTIVE BY ITS NUMBER

In the following pages are listed all steam locomotives at present running on the British Railways' nationalised system, arranged, as far as possible in order of number.

This method will ensure quick and easy reference to any locomotive observed.

The numbers shown under each photograph indicate the range over which engines of any particular class may be found, but it does not necessarily infer that all the numbers belong to one type of engine, or that they run continuously. This is particularly the case with the former Southern Railway engines (numbered in the 30000's), and even where a block of numbers is allocated exclusively to one class there are likely to be many gaps owing to some of the engines being no longer in existence.

In pre-grouping days the old Midland Railway was the only one which had adopted a really satisfactory and logical system of numbering its locomotives, all those of one class being grouped consecutively in one series, but at the grouping this method was adopted for the whole of the L.M.S.R. In 1946 the L.N.E.R., which had a very mixed and largely haphazard numbering inherited from its former constituents, completely renumbered its locomotive stock somewhat on the lines of the L.M.S. system.

Identification of locomotives by the number alone, therefore, will be a simple matter, particularly of those numbered above 40000, as these almost without exception run in complete blocks of numbers allocated to each class. In the case of the lower numbers it is not quite so straightforward, as the former Great Western Railway's somewhat peculiar numbering system does not lend itself readily to listing in strict numerical order, and the Southern had never re-numbered its locomotives apart from the original plan, which at least had the merit of retaining the engine's identity with its pre-grouping number. In the case of those numbered in the 30000's, 31000's and 32000's, therefore, the classes are placed in the most convenient order which should result in identification of a particular locomotive as easily as possible.

With regard to engines numbered between 1000 and 9999, the order of presentation is governed by the second figure (i.e. the *hundreds*, not the *thousands*), resulting from the G.W.R.'s system of grouping the numbers of various classes by this method. This plan will be more readily understood from the table below, which indexes the pages on which the various groups of numbers may be found.

A few odd locomotives, usually ones specially allocated to departmental duties, are not included in the ordinary running stock. Engines on the Isle of Wight are also numbered in a separate series. Particulars of all of these are also listed below, showing the pages on which reference to these may be found.

ENGINES NUMBERED BELOW 9999

B.R. Engines with odd numbers out of series

"VALE OF RHEIDOL" CLASS   2–6–2T

7, 8, 9

Origin: Vale of Rheidol Railway.
Introduced: 1902.
Driving Wheel: 2 ft. 6in.

*Cylinders (2): 11½ in. × 17 in.
Gauge: 1 ft. 11½ in.
Boiler Pressure: 165 lb.sq.in.
*Tractive Effort: 10,510 lb.

Number Series: 7, 8, 9.

Historical Notes: Built specially for working the narrow gauge line between Aberystwyth and Devils Bridge. This is now the only narrow gauge line owned by British Railways, and is open for passenger service during the summer months. No. 9, "Prince of Wales", is one of two engines supplied to the original line in 1902. No. 7, "Owain Glyndwr", and 8, "Llywelyn", were built to the same design by the G.W.R. on taking over the line in 1923.

* The original engine No. 9 has 11 in. × 17 in. cylinders and T.E. 9,615 lb.

49

Origin: Great North of Scotland Railway.
Introduced: 1920.
Driving Wheel: 6 ft. 1 in.

Cylinders (2): 18 in. × 26 in.
Boiler Pressure: 165 lb. sq. in.
Tractive Effort: 16,185 lb.

Number and Name: 49, "Gordon Highlander".

Historical Notes: Last survivor of a class of eight engines built in 1920 for express work on the old G.N.O.S.R. Withdrawn in 1958 as B.R. 62277, now restored to its original condition and livery for working special trains.

Location: When not in use is normally kept at Keith.

103

Origin: Highland Railway.
Introduced: 1894.
Driving Wheel: 5 ft. 3 in.
Cylinders (2): 20 in. × 26 in.

Boiler Pressure: 175 lb. sq. in.
Tractive Effort: 24,555 lb.

Number Series: 103.

Historical Notes: The first 4–6–0 engine in the British Isles. Fifteen of the class were built by the Highland Railway in 1894, numbered 103–117. The last to run in ordinary service was No. 112, withdrawn in 1940 as L.M.S. No. 17925. No. 103, then L.M.S. No. 17916, was taken out of service in 1934 and repainted in H.R. green for preservation. In 1959 it was restored to working order for service with special trains, at the same time acquiring the Stroudly yellow livery formerly in use on the Highland Railway.

Location: When not in use is normally kept at Dawsholm.

123

Origin: Caledonian Railway
Introduced: 1886.
Driving Wheel: 7 ft.
Cylinders (2): 18 in. × 26 in.

Boiler Pressure: 150 lb. sq. in.
Tractive Effort: 12,785 lb.

Number Series: 123.

Historical Notes: Built in 1886 by Messrs. Neilson & Co. for the Caledonian Railway. Took part in the Race to the North in 1888. During the 1920's it was allocated to working the Directors' saloon, but in 1930 was returned to ordinary service and ran until 1935, being then the last single-wheeled express engine running in the country. It was then L.M.S. No. 14010. On withdrawal it was repainted in the old C.R. colours for preservation, and in 1958 was restored to working order for service with special trains.

Location: When not in use is normally kept at Dawsholm.

256

Origin: North British Rail-
   way.
Introduced: 1913.
Driving Wheel: 6 ft.

Cylinders (2): 20 in. × 26 in.
Boiler Pressure: 165 lb. sq.
   in.
Tractive Effort: 20,260 lb.

Number Series: 256 ("Glen Douglas").

Historical Notes: One of a class of 32 built by the North
British Railway, many of which did much service on the
West Highland line.   Withdrawn in 1959 as B.R. No.
62469, now restored to its original condition and livery for
working special trains.   A number of the rest of the class are
still in ordinary service (see page 171).

Location: When not in use is normally kept at Keith.

1000

Origin: Midland Railway.
Introduced: 1902.
Driving Wheel: 7 ft.
Cylinders:
   2 low pressure, 21 in. ×
   26 in.

1 high pressure, 19 in. ×
26 in.
Boiler Pressure: 200 lb. sq.
in.
Tractive Effort: 21,840 lb.

Number Series: 1000.

Historical Notes: The first of Johnson's well-known 3-cylinder compounds for the Midland Railway. The design was later modified by Deeley and eventually totalled 240 engines constructed by the M.R. and L.M.S. Companies (see page 107). On withdrawal in 1951 as B.R. No. 41000 it was retained for preservation and in 1959 was restored in working order to its 1914 condition for use with special trains.

Location: When not in use is normally kept at Derby.

"COUNTY" ("10xx") CLASS   4-6-0

1000–1029

Origin: G.W.R.
Introduced: Aug., 1945.
Driving Wheel: 6 ft. 3 in.
Bogie Wheel: 3 ft.
Length: 63 ft. 0¼ in.
Total Weight: 125 tons 17 cwt.
Water Capacity: 4,000 gals.
Designer: F. W. Hawksworth.

Purpose: Fast Mixed **Traffic.**
Cylinders (2): 18½ in. × 30 in.
Boiler Pressure: 280 lb.sq.in.
Tractive Effort: 32,580 lb.
Coal Capacity: 7 tons.
Power Classification: 6–MT.
Route Availability: Red.
G.W. Power Class: D.

Additional Identification Features: Boiler strongly tapered from fire-box crown to smoke-box. One flat-topped splasher over all driving-wheels on each side. Cylinders set between bogie-wheels, and steam pipes to the smoke-box are straight. Glazed side-windows to cab. Some have double chimneys.

Number Series: 1000 to 1029.

Location: Found on most routes of the former **G.W.R.** main line.

4037, 4073–4099, 5000–5099, 7000–7037

Origin: G.W.R.
Introduced: Aug., 1923.
Driving Wheel: 6 ft. 8½ in.
Bogie Wheel: 3 ft. 2 in.
Length: 65 ft. 2 in.
Total Weight: 126 tons 11 cwt.
Water Capacity: 4,000 gals.
Designer: C. B. Collett.

Purpose: Express Passenger.
Cylinders (4): 16 in. × 26 in.
Boiler Pressure: 225 lb. sq. in.
Tractive Effort: 31,625 lb.
Coal Capacity: 6 tons.
Power Classification: 7–P.
G.W. Power Class: D.
Route Availability: Red.

Additional Identification Features: Several of the class are now fitted with double chimneys.

Number Series: 4037, 4073 to 4099, 5000 to 5099, and 7000 to 7037, with gaps due to scrapping.

Historical Notes: One of the most successful locomotives ever built for any railway. Caerphilly Castle, the first engine of this class, appeared at the Empire Exhibition in 1924. On June 8, 1932, No. 5006 covered the 77¼ miles from Swindon to London in 56½ minutes, 39 miles of the run being made at an average of 90 m.p.h. No. 4037 is a conversion from the earlier "Star" class.

Location: Found on most routes of the former G.W.R. main line.

"KING" (60xx) CLASS   4-6-0

6000–6029

Origin: G.W.R.
Introduced: 1927.
Driving Wheel: 6 ft. 6 in.
Bogie Wheel: 3 ft.
Length: 68 ft. 2 in.
Total Weight: 135 tons 14 cwt.
Water Capacity: 4,000 gals.
Designer: C. B. Collett.

Purpose: Express Passenger.
Cylinders (4): 16¼ in. × 28 in.
Boiler Pressure: 250 lb. sq. in.
Tractive Effort: 40,300 lb.
Coal Capacity: 6 tons.
Power Classification: 8–P.
Route Availability: Double Red.
G.W. Power Class: Special.

Additional Identification Features: All of the class have latterly acquired double chimneys.

Number Series: 6000 to 6029.

Historical Notes: Development by Collett of the "Castle" class (*q.v.*) upon which they were a considerable advance, having a larger boiler. Employed on such trains as the "Cornish Riviera Limited", the first of the class was exhibited in America in 1927 at the Baltimore and Ohio Railroad Centenary Celebrations, where its high power for small size greatly impressed American engineers. No. 6000 ("King George V") was presented with an American locomotive bell by the B. and O. authorities, which the engine still carries over the front buffer-beam.

Location: Employed on the G.W.R. main lines from Paddington to Plymouth, Bristol and Birmingham.

9014, 9017

Origin: G.W.R.
Introduced: 1936.
Driving Wheel: 5 ft. 8 in.
Bogie Wheel: 3 ft. 8 in.
Length: 56 ft. 1¾ in.
Weight: 89 tons.
Water Capacity: 3,500 gals.
Designer: C. B. Collett (re-build).

Purpose: Light Passenger.
Cylinders (2): 18 in. × 26 in.
Boiler Pressure: 180 lb.sq.in.
Tractive Effort: 18,955 lb.
Coal Capacity: 6 tons.
Power Classification: 2–P.
Route Availability: Yellow.
G.W. Power Class: B.

Additional Identification Features: Very low-built engines with tall chimney and dome tapered, brass casing to safety-valve mounted on top of flat-topped Belpaire fire-box. Outside frames and springs to bogie. Springs to front driving-wheels placed above footplate level. Outside straight frames used throughout.

Number Series: Originally 9000–9028, from which two survivors only remain.

Historical Notes: A rebuild incorporating the frames of the older "Bulldog" ("3300" class) and the "Duke" ("3252" class) type of boiler. Twenty-nine engines were thus rebuilt with parallel domed boilers.

Location: North Wales on the former Cambrian Railway lines.

1143

Origin: Swansea Harbour Trust.
Introduced: 1906.
Driving Wheel: 3 ft. 7 in.

Cylinders (2): 15 in. $\times$ 21 in.
Boiler Pressure: 150 lb. sq. in.
Tractive Effort: 14,010 lb.

Number: 1143.

Historical Notes: Acquired by the G.W.R. in 1923 from the Swansea Harbour Trust.

Location: Latterly used for shunting at Clee Hill, near Shrewsbury.

1151, 1152

Origin: Messrs. Powlesland & Mason.
Introduced: 1907.
Driving Wheel: 3 ft. 7 in.

Cylinders (2): 15 in. × 21 in.
Boiler Pressure: 150 lb. sq. in.
Tractive Effort: 14,010 lb.

Number Series: 1151, 1152.

Historical Notes: Acquired by the G.W.R. in 1923 from Messrs. Powlesland & Mason, Swansea.

Location: Shunters in Swansea docks.

"51xx," "61xx" and "81xx" CLASSES*
2-6-2T

4100–4179, 5100–5199, 6100–6169, 8100–8109

Origin: G.W.R.
Introduced: 1906.
Driving Wheel: 5 ft. 8 in.
Pony Wheel: 3 ft. 2 in.
Trailing Wheel: 3 ft. 8 in.
Length: 41 ft.
Weight: 78 tons 9 cwt.
Water Capacity: 2,000 gals.
Designers: Churchward and Collett.
Purpose: Suburban Passenger.

Cylinders (2): 18 in. × 30 in.
Boiler Pressure: 225 lb. sq. in. (61xx), others 200 lb.
Tractive Effort: 23,000 lb. (61xx), 28,165 lb. (81xx) others 24,300 lb.
Coal Capacity: 4 tons.
Power Classification: 4–MT.
Route Availability: Blue.
G.W. Power Class: D.

Additional Identification Features: Footplate raised from front of cylinders to cab doors. Tapered boiler with square firebox. No dome, but tapering safety-valve casing in its place. Back of bunker curved outwards over rear buffers.

Number Series: 4100–4179, 5100–5199, 6100–6169, 8100–8109, with gaps due to scrapping.

Location: Suburban work on most parts of the former G.W.R. system.

* Three separate classes are included here, all of similar appearance and with slight variations in dimensions.

"22xx" ("2251") CLASS

0–6–0

2200–2299, 3200–3219

Origin: G.W.R.
Introduced: March, 1930.
Driving Wheel: 5 ft. 2 in.
Length: 53 ft. 8¼ in.
*Weight: 43 tons 8 cwt.
Water Capacity: 3,000 gals.
Designer: C. B. Collett.
Purpose: Medium Freight and Passenger.

Cylinders (2): 17½ in. × 24 in.
Boiler Pressure: 200 lb.sq.in.
Tractive Effort: 20,155 lb.
Coal Capacity: 5 tons.
Power Classification: 3–MT.
Route Availability: Yellow.
G.W. Power Class: B.

Additional Identification Features: Short tapered boiler with projecting smoke-box. No dome. Safety-valves incorporated in top-feed on the back ring of boiler. Flat-topped fire-box. Cab fitted with one window on each side.

Number Series: 2200 to 2299 and 3200 to 3219, with gaps due to scrapping.

Location: Seen on freight work and stopping passenger trains over most parts of the former G.W.R. system.

* Tender extra, 36 tons 15 cwt. (with R.O.D. tender, 47 tons 14 cwt.).

4200–4299, 5200–5264

Origin: G.W.R.
Introduced: Dec., 1910 and June, 1923.
Driving Wheel: 4 ft. 7½ in.
Pony Wheel: 3 ft. 2 in.
Length: 40 ft. 9 in.
Weight: 81 tons 12 cwt. (42xx), 82 tons 2 cwt. (52xx).
Water Capacity: 1,800 gals.
Designer: George Churchward.

Purpose: Heavy coal traffic.
Cylinders (2): 18½ in. × 30 in. (42xx), 19 in. × 30 in. (52xx).
Boiler Pressure: 200 lb. sq. in.
Tractive Effort: 31,450 lb. (42xx), 33,170 (52xx).
Route Availability: Red.
G.W. Power Class: E.
Power Class: 7-F (42xx), 8-F (52xx).

Additional Identification Features: The only 2-8-0 tank classes on British Railways.

Number Series: 4200–4299 and 5200–5264, with gaps due to scrapping and rebuilding into 7200 class.

Historical Notes: The "52xx" class ("5205" class), was a development of the earlier "4200's", with larger cylinders and other minor alterations. The forty built between December, 1925 and October, 1930 which were numbered 5255 and 5294 are now running as 2-8-2T Class "72xx". The present Nos. 5255 to 5264 were built between January and March, 1940.

Location: Heavy freight work on the former G.W.R. system, principally in South Wales.

41

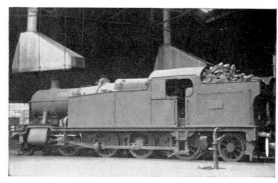

7200–7253

Origin: G.W.R.
Introduced: Aug., 1934.
Driving Wheel: 4 ft. 7½ in.
Pony Wheel: 3 ft. 2 in.
Trailing Wheel: 3 ft. 8 in.
Length: 44 ft. 10 in.
Weight: 92 tons 12 cwt.
Water Capacity: 2,500 gals.
Designer: C. B. Collett.

Purpose: Heavy Main-line Coal Traffic.
Cylinders (2): 19 in. × 30 in.
Boiler Pressure: 200 lb.sq.in.
Tractive Effort: 33,170 lb.
Coal Capacity: 6 tons.
Route Availability: Red.
G.W. Power Class: E.
Power Class: 8–F.

Additional Identification Features: The only 2–8–2 tank class on British Railways. Distinguishable from the "42xx" and "52xx" classes by wheel arrangement.

Number Series: 7200 to 7253.

Historical Notes: These engines were conversions by Mr. Collett of the "42xx" class, rebuilt with larger bunker and fitted with a radial trailing truck. The first twenty (later 5275 to 5294) had never done any mileage as 2–8–0T apart from trials, and became 7200 to 7219 when converted to 2–8–2T.

Location: Heavy freight work on the former G.W.R. system. Principally in South Wales.

"CARDIFF RAILWAY" CLASS   0–4–0ST

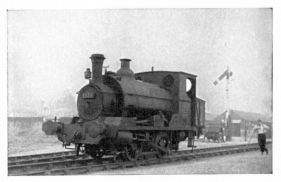

1338

Origin: Cardiff Railway.
Introduced: 1893.
Driving Wheel: 3 ft. 2½ in.

Cylinders (2): 14 in. × 21 in.
Boiler Pressure: 160 lb. sq. in.
Tractive Effort: 14,540 lb.

Additional Identification Features: Unusual type of valve-gear.

Historical Notes: Built by Kitsons for the Cardiff Railway, and the last remaining engine taken over from that line.

Location: Shunts in the Swansea area.

0–6–0ST

1361–1365

Origin: G.W.R.
Introduced: 1910.
Purpose: Dock Shunting.
Weight: 35¼ tons.

Driving Wheel: 3 ft. 8 in.
Cylinders (2): 16 in. × 20 in.
Boiler Pressure: 150 lb.
Tractive Effort: 14,835 lb.

Additional Identification Features: Distinguished from "1366" class by round saddle tanks.

Number Series: 1361 to 1365.

Historical Notes: Designed by Churchward for shunting in sidings where there are severe curves, as usually in docks.

Location: One at Laira (Plymouth), two at Swindon, one allocated to Taunton, but often found at Bridgwater and one at Weymouth.

0–6–0PT

1366–1371

Origin: G.W.R.
Introduced: 1934.
Purpose: Dock Shunting.
Weight: 35¾ tons.

Driving Wheel: 3 ft. 8 in.
Cylinders (2): 16 in. × 20 in.
Boiler Pressure: 165 lb. sq. in.
Tractive Effort: 16,320 lb.

Additional Identification Features: Distinguished from "1361" class by square pannier tanks.

Number Series: 1366 to 1371. No. 1370 has been scrapped.

Historical Notes: A development by Collett of Churchward's "1361" class.

Location: One at Taunton (sometimes to be found at Bridgwater), one at Swindon, and three at Weymouth. One of the latter works the Channel Islands Boat Trains through the streets of Weymouth to the quayside.

"43xx" CLASS

2-6-0

5300–5399, 6300–6399, 7300–7341

Origin: G.W.R.
Introduced: 1911.
Driving Wheel: 5 ft. 8 in.
Pony Wheel: 3 ft. 2 in.
Length: 58 ft. 7¼ in.
•Weight: 102 tons.
Water Capacity: 3,500 gals.
Designer: G. J. Churchward.
Purpose: Mixed Traffic.

Cylinders (2)*:* 18½ in. × 30 in.
Boiler Pressure: 200 lb. sq. in.
Tractive Effort: 25,670 lb.
Coal Capacity: 6 tons.
Power Classification: 4–MT.
Route Availability: Blue
("93xx" Class : Red).
G.W. Power Class: D.

Additional Identification Features: Nos. 7322–7341 have side-window cabs.

Number Series: 5300–5399, 6300–6399, with gaps due to scrapping, and 7300–7341.

Historical Notes: Introduced in 1911, the class originally included Nos. 4300–4399, but all of this earlier series are now scrapped.

Location: Seen on mixed traffic work on almost all parts of the former G.W.R. system.

* Nos. 7322–7341 weigh 105 tons 6 cwt.

"1400" CLASS 0–4–2T

1400–1474

Origin: G.W.R.
Introduced: Aug., 1932.
Driving Wheel: 5 ft. 2 in.
Trailing Wheel: 3 ft. 8 in.
Length: 29 ft. 11 in.
Weight: 41 tons 6 cwt.
Water Capacity: 800 gals.
Designer: C. B. Collett.

Purpose: Light Branch Traffic.
Cylinders (2): 16 in. × 24 in.
Boiler Pressure: 165 lb. sq. in.
Tractive Effort: 13,900 lb.
Coal Capacity: 2 tons 13 cwt.
Power Classification: 1–P.
Route Availability: All Routes.
G.W. Power Class: Unclassed.

Additional Identification Features: Straight footplate. Tall chimney and dome. Tapering safety-valve casing mounted on flat-topped fire-box.

Number Series: 1400 to 1474, with gaps due to scrapping.

Historical Notes: The "1400" class was, when introduced, known as the "4800" class and was fitted for "push-pull" working. They replaced an older but somewhat similar design of 0–4–2T built in the 1870's and 1880's.

Location: Branch lines on the former G.W.R. system. Usually employed on motor (push and pull) trains.

3400–3409, 8400–8499, 9400–9499

Origin: G.W.R.
Introduced: Feb., 1947.
Driving Wheel: 4 ft. 7½ in.
Weight: 55 tons 7 cwt.
Designer: F. W. Hawksworth.
Purpose: Heavy Shunting.

Cylinders (2): 17½ in. × 24 in.
Boiler Pressure: 200 lb.sq.in.
Tractive Effort: 22,515 lb.
Power Classification: 4–F.
Route Availability: Red.
G.W Power Class: C.

Additional Identification Features: Very sturdily-built pannier tank locomotive. Taper boiler with G.W.R. fittings.

Number Series: (Introduced 1947): Nos. 9400 to 9409.*
(Introduced 1950): 8400 to 8499, 9410 to 9499, and 3400–3409, with gaps due to scrapping.

Historical Notes: Although of quite recent construction, many of these engines have already been made redundant owing to Dieselisation, and have been taken out of service.

Location: Seen on all parts of the former G.W.R. system, on shunting, short distance freight and passenger duties. Nos. 8400–8406 are stationed at Bromsgrove on the former L.M.S. system, and are used for banking on the Lickey Incline.

* Nos. 9400–9409 have superheaters.

3440

Origin: G.W.R.
Introduced: 1901.
Driving Wheel: 6 ft. 8½ in.
Bogie Wheel: 3 ft. 8 in.
Length: 56 ft. 4¾ in.
Designer: William Dean.

Cylinders (2): 18. in × 26 in.
Boiler Pressure: 200 lb. sq. in.
Tractive Effort: 17,790 lb.
Water Capacity: 3,000 gals.
Coal Capacity: 5 tons.
Route Availability: Red.
Power Classification: (G.W.R.)
A; (B.R.) 3-P.

Additional Identification Features: Outside frames, painted brown. Tender lined out in three panels with 'G.W.R.' monogram in centre. Standard taper boiler and other usual G.W.R. features.

Number Series: 3440 "City of Truro." From 1912 until 1937 it carried the number 3717, but has now reverted to its original 3440.

Historical Notes: One of a series of ten engines constructed in 1903 and named after cities. It was the 2000th engine built at Swindon. The first engine in this country to be recorded as having attained a speed of over 100 m.p.h., which it achieved in 1904 on Wellington Bank when working a special boat train from Plymouth to Paddington. Withdrawn from service in 1931 and preserved in York Museum until early 1957, when it was renovated and put back into traffic, being repainted in the old G.W.R. style of the early part of the century.

Location: When not in use is normally kept at Swindon.

5400–5424, 6400–6439, 7400–7449

Origin: G.W.R.
Introduced: Feb., 1932.
•*Driving Wheel:* 4 ft. 7½ in.
Length: 31 ft. 1 in.
Weight: 45 tons 12 cwt.
Water Capacity: 1,100 gals.
Designer: C. B. Collett.
Purpose: Light Passenger Work.

Cylinders (2): 16½ in. × 24 in.
•*Boiler Pressure:* 165 lb. sq. in.
•*Tractive Effort:* 16,510 lb.
Coal Capacity: 3 tons 4 cwt.
Power Classification: 2–P.
Route Availability: Yellow.
G.W. Power Class: A.

Additional Identification Features: The 5400's and 6400's are fitted for pull and push working, but the 7400's are not motor fitted.

Number Series: 5400–5424 (with gaps due to scrapping), 6400–6439, 7400–7449.

Location: On various parts of the former G.W.R. system on branch lines and short distance local passenger trains.

• The 5400 series have 5 ft. 2 in. wheels and a tractive effort of 14,780 lb. The 7400's have 180 lb. boiler pressure and a tractive effort of 18,010 lb.

1500–1509

Origin: B.R.
Introduced: June, 1949.
Driving Wheel: 4 ft. 7½ in.
Length: 33 ft.
Weight: 58 tons 4 cwt.
Water Capacity: 1,350 gals.
Designer: F. W. Hawksworth.

Purpose: Heavy Shunting Work on Restricted Curves.
Cylinders (2): 17½ in. × 24 in.
Boiler Pressure: 200 lb.sq.in.
Tractive Effort: 22,515 lb.
Power Classification: 4–F.
Route Availability: Red.
G.W. Power Class: C.

Additional Identification Features: Absence of footplate. Outside cylinders set well forward. Walschaert valve gear. Sloping steampipes at side of smoke-box. Pannier tanks do not flank sides of smoke-box.

Number Series: Nos. 1500 to 1509. No. 1509 has been scrapped.

Historical Notes: Specially designed to be able to haul heavy freight trains and shunt in goods yards on track of a minimum radius of three chains. For this reason the fixed wheel-base is set at 12 ft. 10 in.

Location: Seen only in the London and Newport areas.

"45xx" CLASS

4500–4599, 5500–5574

Origin: G.W.R.
Introduced: 1906.
Driving Wheel: 4 ft. 7½ in.
Pony Wheel: 3 ft. 2 in.
Trailing Wheel: 3 ft. 2 in.
Length: 36 ft. 4½ in.
*Weight: 57 tons.
*Water Capacity: 1,000 gals.
Designer: George Churchward.

Purpose: Passenger (Light Branch).
Cylinders (2): 17 in. × 24 in.
Boiler Pressure: 200 lb. sq. in.
Tractive Effort: 21,250 lb.
Coal Capacity: 3 tons 14 cwt.
Route Availability: Yellow.
Power Classification: 4–MT.
G.W. Power Class: C.

Additional Identification Features: Straight footplate only very slightly raised at front end of cylinders. A much shorter and smaller-built engine than the other classes of G.W.R. 2–6–2T. Nos. 4575 onwards * have larger tanks with sloping tops.

Number Series: 4500–4599, and 5500–5574, with gaps due to scrapping. Most of the earlier engines below 4555 have now disappeared.

Location: Seen on most parts of the former G.W.R. system, except the London area.

* Nos. 4575 onwards: water capacity 1,300 gals., weight 61 tons.

1600–1669

Origin: B.R.
Introduced: Oct., 1949.
Driving Wheel: 4 ft. 1½ in.
Weight: 41 tons 12 cwt.
Designer: F. W. Hawksworth.
Purpose: Shunting and Branch-line.

Cylinders (2)*:* 16½ in. × 24 in.
Boiler Pressure: 165 lb.sq.in.
Tractive Effort: 18,515 lb.
Power Classification: 2–F.
Route Availability: All routes.
G.W. Power Class: A.

Additional Identification Features: Noticeably smaller than most other G.W.R. Pannier tanks. Very small splashers. Number Series should be used for identification.

Number Series: 1600 to 1669, with gaps due to scrapping. Although of recent construction, several have already been made redundant by Dieselisation.

Historical Notes: A development of the old "1901" and "2021" classes of 1881 and 1897.

Location: Branch lines on the former G.W.R. system. Several are stationed at Lydney and also at Burry Port.

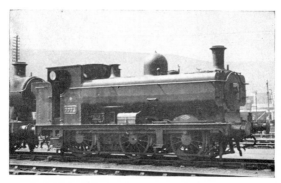

3600–3799, 4600–4699, 5700–5799, 6700–6779,
7700–7799, 8700–8799, 9600–9682, 9711–9799

Origin: G.W.R.
Introduced: 1929.
Driving Wheel: 4 ft. 7½ in.
Length: 31 ft. 2 in.
Weight: 50 tons (approx.).
Water Capacity: 1,200 gals.
Designer: C. B. Collett.
Purpose: Shunting and Light
 Freight.

Cylinders (2): 17½ in. × 24 in.
Boiler Pressure: 200 lb. sq. in.
Tractive Effort: 22,515 lb.
Coal Capacity: 3 tons 6 cwt.
Power Classification: 4–F.
Route Availability: Yellow (y).
G.W. Power Class: C.

Additional Identification Features: The later built engines
have modified cabs.

Number Series: 3600–3799, 4600–4699, 5700–5799, 6700–6779,
7700–7799, 8700–8799, 9600–9682, 9711–9799, with gaps due to
scrapping.

Historical Notes: Became the standard G.W.R. shunting and
general purpose tank engine from 1929 onwards. Often seen on
passenger trains, except 6700–6779 which are not vacuum fitted.

Location: This extremely numerous class is seen all over the
former G.W.R. system.

CONDENSING PANNIER TANK CLASS
0–6–0PT

9700–9710

Origin: G.W.R.
Introduced: 1931.
Driving Wheel: 4 ft. 7½ in.
Length: 31 ft. 2 in.
Weight: 50 tons (approx.).
Water Capacity: 1,200 gals.
Designer: C. B. Collett.
Purpose: For working through the Metropolitan tunnels.

Cylinders (2): 17½ in. × 24 in.
Boiler Pressure: 200 lb.sq.in.
Tractive Effort: 22,515 lb.
Coal Capacity: 3 tons 6 cwt.
Power Classification: 4–F.
Route Availability: Yellow (y).
G.W. Power Class: C.

Additional Identification Features: Distinguished from the standard class by the extended side tanks and condensing pipes.

Number Series: 9700 to 9710.

Historical Notes: A specially adapted version of the standard 5700, fitted with condensing apparatus for tunnel working.

Location: All at Old Oak, and used on freight trains through the Metropolitan tunnels.

5600–5699, 6600–6699

Origin: G.W.R.
Introduced: Dec., 1924.
Driving Wheel: 4 ft. 7½ in.
Trailing Wheel: 3 ft. 8 in.
Length: 37 ft. 6 in.
Weight: 62 tons 18 cwt.
Water Capacity: 1,900 gals.
Designer: C. B. Collett.
Purpose: Mixed Traffic (South Wales).

Cylinders (2): 18 in. × 26 in.
Boiler Pressure: 200 lb.sq.in.
Tractive Effort: 25,800 lb.
Coal Capacity: 3 tons 15 cwt.
Power Classification: 5–MT.
Route Availability: Red.
G.W. Power Class: D.

Additional Identification Features: Exceptional front overhang of boiler and smoke-box gives an unbalanced appearance. Small driving-wheels with only the front splasher visible. Sloping top to side-tanks.

Number Series: ("56xx"): 5600 to 5699. ("66xx"): 6600 to 6699.

Historical Notes: The "66xx" variant was introduced in 1927, and weighed 15 cwt. more than the "56xx"-class engines.

Location: The majority of these engines are located in South Wales, but they are also found in other parts of the G.W.R. system.

4700–4708

Origin: G.W.R.
Introduced: 1919.
Driving Wheel: 5 ft. 8 in.
Pony Wheel: 3 ft. 2 in.
Length: 66 ft. 4¼ in.
*Weight: 82 tons.
Water Capacity: 4,000 gals.
Designer: George Church-ward.

Purpose: Heavy Fast Freight.
Cylinders (2): 19 in. × 30 in.
Boiler Pressure: 225 lb.sq.in.
Tractive Effort: 30,460 lb.
Coal Capacity: 6 tons.
Power Classification: 7-F.
Route Availability: Red.
G.W. Power Classes D.

Additional Identification Features: As "28xx" class (*q.v.*), but with larger driving-wheels and splashers. Larger boiler, drive on second coupled axle, and almost vertical steam-pipes.

Number Series: 4700 to 4708.

Historical Notes: Originally a mixed traffic design. They are classed as route availability–red, which rather limits their usefulness.

Location: Usually seen between London and Bristol or London and Birmingham. Occasionally used on passenger trains.

* Tender extra, 46 tons 14 cwt.

2800–2899, 3800–3866

Origin: G.W.R.
Introduced: 1903.
Driving Wheel: 4 ft. 7½ in.
Pony Wheel: 3 ft. 2 in.
Length: 63 ft. 2½ in.
Weight: 75 tons 10 cwt.
Water Capacity: 3,500 gals.
Designer: George Churchward.

Purpose: Heavy Long-distance Freight.
Cylinders (2): 18½ in. × 30 in.
Boiler Pressure: 225 lb. sq. in.
Tractive Effort: 35,380 lb.
Coal Capacity: 6 tons.
Power Classification: 8–F.
Route Availability: Blue.
G.W. Power Class: E.

Additional Identification Features: General build is long and low. Footplate with very small splashers over driving-wheels. Standard G.W. chimney, safety-valve, and tapered boiler. Outside cylinders. Footplate drops to buffer-beam level at front.

Number Series: Class "28xx" (1903): 2800 to 2883, with gaps due to scrapping. Class "2884" (1938): 2884 to 2899 and 3800 to 3866.

Historical Notes: In 1938 C. B. Collett introduced a variant of this class (the "2884" class), which had side windows to their cabs and other small alterations.

Location: Heavy freight work on former G.W.R. main lines.

"5800" CLASS

0–4–2T

5815

Origin: G.W.R.
Introduced: 1932.
Driving Wheel: 5 ft. 2 in.
Trailing Wheel: 3 ft. 8 in.
Length: 29 ft. 11 in.
Weight: 41 tons 6 cwt.
Water Capacity: 800 gals.
Designer: C. B. Collett.
Purpose: Light branch work.

Cylinders (2): 16 in. × 24 in.
Boiler Pressure: 165 lb. sq. in.
Tractive Effort: 13,900 lb.
Coal Capacity: 2 tons 13 cwt.
Power Classification: 1–P.
Route Availability: All routes.
G.W. Power Class: Unclassed.

Additional Identification Features: Similar to "1400" class, but not motor-fitted for push and pull working.

Number Series: 5800 to 5819, of which only No. 5815 now remains.

Location: Branch lines on the former G.W.R. system.

6800–6879

Origin: G.W.R.
Introduced: Aug., 1936.
Driving Wheel: 5 ft. 8 in.
Bogie Wheel: 3 ft.
Length: 63 ft. ¼ in.
Weight: 114 tons.
Water Capacity: 3,500 gals.
Designer: C. B. Collett.
Purpose: Fast Freight and Intermediate Passenger.

Cylinders (2): 18½ in. × 30 in.
Boiler Pressure: 225 lb.sq.in.
Tractive Effort: 28,875 lb.
Coal Capacity: 6 tons.
Power Classification: 5–MT.
Route Availability: Red.
G.W. Power Class: D.

Additional Identification Features: Cab as "Castle" class with side-windows. Similar to "Hall" class, but with smaller coupled wheels and footplate raised over cylinders.

Number Series: 6800 to 6879.

Historical Notes: Conversions from the old "4300" class of 2–6–0's built by Churchward from 1911 onwards. New cylinders were fitted, but the original wheels were retained, boiler pressure being raised from 200 to 225 lb. sq. in. Named after famous Granges on the W. Region.

Location: Seen on most parts of the former G.W.R. system.

"MANOR" ("78xx") CLASS 4–6–0

7800–7829

Origin: G.W.R.
Introduced: Jan., 1938.
Driving Wheel: 5 ft. 8 in.
Bogie Wheel: 3 ft.
Length: 61 ft. 9¼ in.
Weight: 108 tons 18 cwt.
Water Capacity: 3,600 gals.
Designer: C. B. Collett.

Purpose: Mixed Traffic for Secondary Lines.
Cylinders (2): 18 in. × 30 in.
Boiler Pressure: 225 lb.sq.in.
Tractive Effort: 27,340 lb.
Coal Capacity: 6 tons.
Power Classification: 5—MT.
Route Availability: Blue.
G.W. Power Class: D.

Additional Identification Features: Footplate same as "Grange" class (*q.v.*), but not so deep. Cylinders set between bogie-wheels.

Number Series: 7800 to 7829.

Historical Notes: Designed as a general purpose class with light-axle loading enabling work to be done over routes barred to "Halls" and "Granges". There are now 30 engines in the class, mostly all working on passenger trains. Like the "Granges" these are conversions from the "43xx" class, but they are somewhat lighter than the "Granges".

Location: Seen on most parts of the former G.W.R. system, more particularly on such secondary main lines as those of the former Cambrian Railway.

"HALL" CLASS 4-6-0

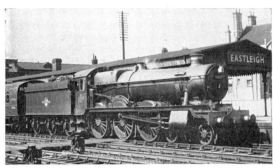

4900–4999, 5900–5999, 6900–6999, 7900–7929

Origin: G.W.R.
Introduced: *
Driving Wheel: 6 ft.
Bogie Wheel: 3 ft.
Length: 63 ft. ¼ in.
Weight: 122½ tons.
Water Capacity: 4,000 gals.
Designer: C. B. Collett.

Purpose: Mixed Traffic.
Cylinders (2): 18½ in. × 30 in.
Boiler Pressure: 225 lb. sq. in.
Tractive Effort: 27,275 lb.
Coal Capacity: 6 tons.
Power Classification: 5–MT.
Route Availability: Red.
G.W. Power Class: D.

Number Series: 4900 to 4910, 4912 to 4999, 5900 to 5999 and 6900 to 6958. Nos. 6959 to 6999 and 7900 to 7929 are "Modified Halls" ("79xx" class). Some have recently been scrapped.

Historical Notes: Designed to provide a powerful general purpose engine. All engines in this class excepting the prototype (No. 4900—"Saint Martin") were introduced in 1928 and were of a modified design for new construction, as distinct from rebuilding. No. 4900 being a rebuild of one of Churchward's 6 ft. 8½ in. "Saint" class. The "79xx" class may be recognised by their different "front-end" and different bogie. No. 4911 was damaged beyond repair in an air raid in 1941 and one or two others, including the original No. 4900, have recently been taken out of service.

Location: A general purpose engine seen on all main lines of the former G.W.R. system.

* No. 4900 Dec., 1924. 4901 onwards, 1928. 6959 onwards, 1944.

"M–7" CLASS   0–4–4T

30021–30676

Origin: L.S.W.R.
Introduced: 1897.
Driving Wheel: 5 ft. 7 in.
Trailing Wheel: 3 ft. 7 in.
Length: 36 ft. 3¼ in.
Weight: 60 tons 4 cwt.
Water Capacity: 1,300 gals.
Designer: Dugald Drummond.

Purpose: Light Passenger Suburban.
Cylinders (2): 18½ in. × 26 in.
Boiler Pressure: 175 lb.sq.in.
Tractive Effort: 19,755 lb.
Coal Capacity: 3 tons.
Power Classification: 2–P.

Additional Identification Features: Some have leading sand-boxes under footplate instead of combined with splashers. Dome with safety-valves mounted on top.

Number Series: 30021 to 30060, 30104 to 30112, 30123-4-5, 31027 to 30133, 30241 to 30256, 30318 to 30324, 30328, 30356-7, 30374 to 30379, 30479 to 30481, 30667 to 30676. A few of the class have recently been scrapped.

Historical Notes: Now includes the original "M–7" engines the "X–14" class (introduced in 1903).

Location: Seen on all parts of the former L.S.W.R. system and on some parts of the old L.B. & S.C.R. Many now fitted for pull and push working.

"U.S.A." CLASS

0-6-0T

30061–30074

Origin: United States of America.
Purchased by S.R.: Dec., 1946.
Driving Wheel: 4 ft. 6 in.
Length: 29 ft. 8 in.
Weight: 46 tons 10 cwt.
Water Capacity: 1,200 U.S. gals.

Designer: U.S. Army Transportation Corps.
Purpose: Heavy-duty Dock Shunting.
Cylinders (2): 16½ in. × 24 in.
Boiler Pressure: 210 lb.sq.in.
Tractive Effort: 21,600 lb.
Coal Capacity: 1 U.S. ton.
Power Classification: 3–F.

Additional Identification Features: A typically American "Switcher" or shunting engine. Stove-pipe chimney and three "domes", the centre one of which carries the whistle. Quite un-English in appearance. Outside cylinders and valve-gear. Connecting-rods drive on rear axle. Very wide cab necessitating special warning notice to shunters riding on steps.

Number Series: 30061 to 30074.

Historical Notes: Fourteen of these engines were purchased by the Southern Railway in 1946 and fitted with altered details for use on English railways.

Location: All of the class work in Southampton Docks.

30089, 30096, 30102

Origin: L.S.W.R.
Introduced: 1891.
Designer: W. Adams.
Purpose: Dock shunting.

Driving wheel: 3 ft. 10. in.
Cylinders (2): 16 in. × 22 in.
Boiler Pressure: 140 lb. sq.in.
Tractive Effort: 14,650 lb.

Additional Identification Features: Some engines had Drummond-type boilers with safety valves on the dome.

Number Series: The class originally ran from 30081 to 30103, 30147, and 30176.

Historical Notes: Designed by Adams for shunting where there are sharp curves. Most of them spent many years in Southampton Docks. The three survivors now have little work remaining for them.

Location: Two at Eastleigh, and one at Guildford for shed pilot duty.

14–36, 30177–30236

Origin: L.S.W.R.
Introduced: 1889.
Driving Wheel: 4 ft. 10 in.
Trailing Wheel: 3 ft.
Length: 30 ft. 8½ in.
•*Weight:* 46 tons 18 cwt.
Water Capacity: 800 gals.
Designer: W. Adams.

Purpose: Light Suburban Passenger.
Cylinders (2): 17½ in. × 24 in.
Boiler Pressure: 160 lb. sq. in.
Tractive Effort: 17,245 lb.
Coal Capacity: 1 ton 10 cwt.
Power Classification: 0–P.

Additional Identification Features: Some engines have safety valves mounted on fire-box, others on top of dome. Very common on Isle of Wight lines, where all have Adams-type boilers, with valves over fire-box (W–35 and W–36 are pull-push fitted).

Number Series: (Introduced 1889): 30177–30236, and W14–W36 with gaps due to scrapping and to renumbering on transfer to Isle of Wight.

Historical Notes: Built at Nine Elms to replace the Beattie well-tank engines on branch-lines and short passenger work. Those used in the Isle of Wight are named after various places served, and have larger bunkers, extended rearwards and upwards, and Westinghouse brake pump on left of smoke-box. (These engines weigh 48 tons 8 cwt.)

Location: Apart from the Isle of Wight engines, the few survivors are mostly in the West of England.

• See Historical Notes.

"G-6" CLASS

30238, 30258, 30266, 30274, 30277, DS 3152

Origin: L.S.W.R.
Introduced: 1894.
Driving Wheel: 4 ft. 10 in.
Length: 30 ft. 8½ in.
Weight: 47 tons 13 cwt.
Water Capacity: 1,000 gals.

Designer: W. Adams.
Purpose: Freight and Shunting.
Cylinders (2): 17½ in. × 24 in.
Boiler Pressure: 160 lb. sq. in.
Tractive Effort: 17,235 lb.
Power Classification: 2–F.

Additional Identification Features: Some engines have the safety valve on the dome.

Number Series: (Introduced in 1894): Nos. 30238, 30258, 30266, 30274/7 and service locomotive No. DS 3152.

Historical Notes: Commenced by Adams and completed to an original total of 34 engines by Dugald Drummond.

Location: Seen on shunting work on the former L.S.W.R. No. DS 3152 shunts at Meldon Quarries, near Okehampton.

30330–30335, 30473–30478, 30482–30491,
30521–30524

Origin: L.S.W.R.
Introduced: Jan., 1914.
Driving Wheel: 6 ft.
Bogie Wheel: 3 ft. 7 in.
Length: 65 ft. 6¼ in.
Total Weight: 137 tons 10 cwt. (approx.).
Water Capacity: 5,000 gals.
Designer: Drummond (since rebuilt), Urie, and Maunsell.

Purpose: Mixed Traffic.
Cylinders (2): 21 in. × 28 in.
Boiler Pressure: 180 (some 175) lb. sq. in.
Tractive Effort: 26,240 (some 25,510) lb.
Coal Capacity: 5 tons.
Power Classification: 4–P 5–F.

Additional Identification Features: (Urie engines.) Very similar to "S–15" Uries, but with shorter chimney and smaller dome.

Number Series: 30330 to 30335, 30473 to 30478, 30482 to 30491 and 30521 to 30524. Most of the 30330 and 30482 series are now scrapped, and also some of the 30473–8 batch.

Historical Notes: 30330–335 are rebuilds of Drummond engines of 1905, 30482–491 built new by Urie in 1914, and the others by Maunsell in 1924.

Location: Seen on express freight and sometimes passenger trains between London and Weymouth, and London and Exeter.

30494, 30495

Origin: L.S.W.R.
Introduced: July, 1921.
Driving Wheel: 5 ft. 1 in.
Bogie Wheel: 3 ft. 7 in.
Length: 42 ft. 10¼ in.
Weight: 95 tons 2 cwt.
Water Capacity: 2,000 gals.
Designer: R. W. Urie.

Purpose: Shunting in "hump" yards.
Cylinders: 22 in. × 28 in.
Boiler Pressure: 180 lb.sq.in.
Tractive Effort: 34,000 lb.
Coal Capacity: 3 tons 10 cwt.
Power Classification: 8–F.

Additional Identification Features: A very unusual type. High-pitched boiler with massive smoke-box. Side-tanks have sloping tops towards front end. Footplate raised over cylinders and valve-gear. Outside cylinders and valve-gear. Stove-pipe chimney.

Number Series: 30492–30495 of which the first two are now scrapped.

Historical Notes: Specially designed for dealing with transfer traffic at the then newly-opened "hump" marshalling yards at Feltham.

Location: Still stationed at Feltham, but now largely displaced by Diesels in the marshalling yard.

"S–15" CLASS 4-6-0

30496–30515, 30823–30847

Origin: L.S.W.R.
Introduced: March, 1920.
Driving Wheel: 5 ft. 7 in.
Bogie Wheel: 3 ft. 7 in.
Length: 65 ft. 6¾ in.
Total Weight: 136 tons 4 cwt.
Water Capacity: 5,000 gals.
Designers: R. W. Urie, and
R. E. L. Maunsell.

Purpose: Freight and Mixed
Traffic.
Cylinders (2): 20½ in. × 28 in.
Boiler Pressure: 180 and 200 lb.
sq. in.
Tractive Effort: 28,200 and
29,855 lb.
Coal Capacity: 5 tons.
Power Classification: 6–F.

Additional Identification Features: (Urie engines): Footplate
raised over driving-wheels, and still further raised over cylinders,
sweeping down from them to front buffer-beam. No splashers.
Normal chimney and dome. Round-topped fire-box and cab
without side-windows. Smoke-screens fitted. (Maunsell
engines): Straight footplate over driving-wheels and cylinders.
Cab with roof and sides merging in a curve. Other details as for
Urie engines.

Number Series: 30496 to 30515 (Urie); 30823 to 30847
(Maunsell).

Historical Notes: The Urie engines were built in 1920–1 and the
Maunsell ones in 1927 and 1936.

Location: Seen on main line freight trains on the Southampton
and West of England main lines. Some of the Maunsell engines
are on the Brighton section, and others are to be seen on local
passenger trains between Salisbury and Exeter.

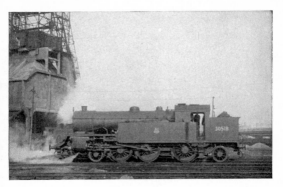

30516–30520

Origin: L.S.W.R.
Introduced: 1921.
Driving Wheel: 5 ft. 7 in.
Bogie Wheel: 3 ft. 7 in.
Length: 46 ft.
Weight: 96 tons 8 cwt.
Water Capacity: 2,000 gals.
Designer: R. W. Urie.

Purpose: Heavy Freight.
Cylinders (2): 21 in. × 28 in.
Boiler Pressure: 180 lb.sq.in.
Tractive Effort: 28,200 lb.
Coal Capacity: 3 tons 10 cwt.
Power Classification: 6–F.

Additional Identification Features: Very similar in outline to "G–16" class (*q.v.*), but tops of side-tanks do not slope down at front end, and coupled wheels are larger.

Number Series: 30516 to 30520.

Historical Notes: Designed for working the interchange traffic between Feltham and Brent and between Feltham and Willesden. They were built immediately after the "G–16's".

Location: Three still stationed at Feltham, engaged on local freight transfer traffic. Nos. 30516 and 30517 now work on the Fawley branch, near Southampton.

30530–30549

Origin: Southern Railway.
Introduced: Jan., 1938.
Driving Wheel: 5 ft. 1 in.
Length: 53 ft. 9½ in.
Total Weight: 90 tons.
Water Capacity: 3,500 gals.
Designer: R. E. L. Maunsell.

Purpose: Freight.
Cylinders (2): 19 in. × 26 in.
Boiler Pressure: 200 lb.sq.in.
Tractive Effort: 26,157 lb.
Coal Capacity: 5 tons.
Power Classification: 4–F.

Additional Identification Features: Straight footplate.
Flat-topped Belpaire fire-box. Large flat-topped dome and
large, squat chimney. Fitted with double blast pipes and
wide chimneys. Side-window to cab in front of cut-away.

Number Series: 30530 to 30549.

Historical Notes: They were the last class to be designed
by Mr. Maunsell before his retirement. Although primarily
intended for freight duties, they are fitted with steam-heat
connections for working passenger trains when required.

Location: Mostly centred on Eastleigh, Bournemouth,
Horsham and Norwood Junction.

30582–30584

Origin: L.S.W.R.
Introduced: 1882.
Designer: W. Adams.
Purpose: Suburban Passenger.

Driving Wheels: 5 ft. 7 in.
Cylinders (2): 17½ in. × 24 in.
BoilerPressure: 160 lb. sq. in.
Tractive Effort: 14,920 lb.

Additional Identification Features: A somewhat distinctive design with very small side tanks. Additional water capacity is provided by well tanks between the frames. One boiler, which is changed from time to time between the three engines, has safety-valves on the fire-box and a tall dome.

Number Series: 30582 to 30584.

Historical Notes: Survivors of a once numerous class, specially retained for working the Lyme Regis branch which abounds in sharp curves, for which the flexible wheel base of these engines has been found to be the most suitable type.

Location: One engine works for a week at a time on the Lyme Regis branch, the other two being kept as spares at Exmouth Junction.

30585–30587

Origin: L.S.W.R.
Built: 1874–5 to a design dating back some years earlier.
Designer: W. Beattie.
Purpose: Suburban Passenger.

Driving Wheels: 5 ft. 7 in.
Cylinders (2): 16½ in. × 20 in.
Boiler Pressure: 160 lb.
Tractive Effort: 11,050 lb.

Additional Identification Features: No. 30586 has square front splashers. The other two have the curved ones as illustrated.

Number Series: 30585 to 30587.

Historical Notes: Survivors of a class which once worked on the London suburban services. These three engines are specially retained for working the Wenford Bridge mineral branch in Cornwall, over which no heavier engines are allowed. They are the oldest *design* still in use on British Railways (although not quite the oldest engines. See page 99), and have been extensively renewed during the course of their career. They have outlasted all their sisters by more than half a century. Very occasionally they may be found working a local passenger train in the Wadebridge area.

Location: Stationed at Wadebridge, Cornwall.

30306–30368, 30687–30701

Origin: L.S.W.R.
Introduced: 1897.
Driving Wheel: 5 ft. 1 in.
Length: 54 ft. 1¼ in.
Total Weight: 86 tons 6 cwt.
Water Capacity: 3,500 gals.
Designer: Dugald Drummond.

Purpose: Freight.
Cylinders (2): 19 in. × 26 in.
Boiler Pressure: 180 lb.sq.in.
Tractive Effort: 23,500 lb.
Coal Capacity: 4 tons.
Power Classification: 3–F.

Additional Identification Features: Straight footplate.
Centre splasher complete, but front one merged with sand-
box and rear one with cab front. Stove-pipe chimney
mounted on extended circular smoke-box, and normal
dome with safety-valves mounted on top.

Number Series: 30306, 30308–9, 30315–6–7, 30325–6–7,
30339, 30346, 30350, 30352, 30355, 30368, 30687, 30689 to
30701.

Historical Notes: Built by Messrs. Dubs & Co. of Glasgow. In November, 1920 No. 30316 was rebuilt by Urie
with an "Eastleigh" superheater, but all now carry
Maunsell-type superheaters.

Location: All on the former L.S.W.R. system, principally
at Nine Elms, Feltham, Guildford, Eastleigh, Salisbury and
Exmouth Junction.

30117–30732

Origin: L.S.W.R.
Introduced: 1899.
Driving Wheel: 6 ft. 7 in.
Bogie Wheel: 3 ft. 7 in.
Length: 63 ft. 9 in.
Weight: 96 tons 3 cwt.
Water Capacity: 4,000 gals.

Designer: D. Drummond.
Purpose: Fast Light Passenger.
Cylinders (2): 19 in. × 26 in.
Boiler Pressure: 175 lb. sq. in.
Tractive Effort: 17,670 lb.
Coal Capacity: 5 tons.
Power Classification: 3–P.

Additional Identification Features: "Stove-pipe" chimney and dome with safety-valves mounted on top. Straight footplate. Separate splasher over coupling-rod on earlier locos in class, but those between 30300 and 30338 have wider, plain splashers. Some engines have 6- and others 8-wheeled tenders.

Number Series: The survivors are numbered 30117, 30120, 30287/8, 30300, 30313, 30338, 30707/9, 30715/7–9, 30729.

Historical Notes: This is the famous London and South Western "Greyhound" class. No. 30336, now scrapped, once brought the Plymouth boat express from Templecombe to Waterloo (112½ miles) at an average speed of 65 m.p.h. The oldest express passenger engines still at work. There were originally 66 engines in the class.

Location: Mostly centred on Exmouth Junction. Still to be seen on light main line passenger trains, particularly between Exeter and Padstow.

"KING ARTHUR" (N-15) CLASS   4-6-0

30448–30457, 30763–30806

Origin: L.S.W.R.
Introduced: Sept., 1918.
Driving Wheel: 6 ft. 7 in.
Bogie Wheel: 3 ft. 7 in.
Length: 66 ft. 5¼ in.
Weight: 138 tons 3 cwt. (approx.).
Water Capacity: 5,000 gals.
Designers: R. W. Urie; (Later modified engines) R. E. L. Maunsell.

Purpose: Express Passenger.
Cylinders (2): 20½ in. × 28 in. (Engine 30755 only, 22-in. cyls.)
Boiler Pressure: 180 lb. sq. in.
Tractive Effort: 26,245 lb.
Coal Capacity: 5 tons.
Power Classification: 5-P.

Additional Identification Features: Round-topped fire-box. Single flat-topped splasher over all driving wheels. Some tenders with 6 wheels, others with 8-wheeled bogies.

Number Series: 30448 to 30457, 30763 to 30806, with gaps due to scrapping.

Historical Notes: Original Urie engines were 30736–30755. In February, 1925 Maunsell advanced upon Urie's design and introduced the "N-15" class, of which the engines have a variety of modifications, weights and tractive efforts. The design was closely followed throughout, however, though three differing sizes of cylinders were fitted. The engines introduced in February, 1926 for use on the Central Section had 6-wheeled tenders, and weighed 81 tons 17 cwt. No. 30449 took part in the Darlington Railway Centenary celebrations in July, 1925.

Location: Now all on the West of England and Bournemouth main lines.

"LORD NELSON" CLASS 4–6–0

30850–30865

Origin: Southern Railway.
Introduced: Aug., 1926.
Driving Wheel: 6 ft. 7 in.
Bogie Wheel: 3 ft. 1 in.
Length: 69 ft. 9¾ in.
Weight: 142 tons 6 cwt. (approx.).
Water Capacity: 5,000 gals.

Designer: R. E. L. Maunsell.
Purpose: Express Passenger.
Cylinders (4): 16½ in. × 26 in.
Boiler Pressure: 220 lb.sq.in.
Tractive Effort: 33,510 lb.
Coal Capacity: 5 tons.
Power Classification: 7–P.

Additional Identification Features: Square-topped fire-box sloping down towards cab front. Almost complete rear splasher merges into cab front. Curved nameplate over middle splasher. Multiple-jet chimney, smoke-screens at side of smoke-box.

Number Series: 30850 to 30865.

Historical Notes: A remarkable and original design in which the cranks of the engine are set to give eight power impulses to each revolution instead of the normal four. Eight "puffs" are thus audible at each revolution of the drivers. (This feature does not apply to engine 30865, which gives the usual 4 exhausts per revolution.) No. 30859 ("Lord Hood") has 6 ft. 3 in. driving-wheels, and also varies in tractive effort.

Location: Usually employed between Waterloo and South-ampton and Bournemouth. Frequently used on Southamp-ton Docks boat trains.

30900–30939

Origin: Southern Railway.
Introduced: 1930.
Driving Wheel: 6 ft. 7 in.
Bogie Wheel: 3 ft. 1 in.
Length: 58 ft. 9¾ in.
Weight: 109 tons 10 cwt.
Water Capacity: 4,000 gals.

Designer: R. E. L. Maunsell.
Purpose: Passenger.
Cylinders (3): 16½ in. × 26 in.
Boiler Pressure: 220 lb. sq. in.
Tractive Effort: 25,135 lb.
Coal Capacity: 5 tons.
Power Classification: 5–P.

Additional Identification Features: Nos. 30900–1, 30907, 30909, 30913–15, 30917–21, 30924, 30929–31, 30933–4, 30937–9 are fitted with multiple jet chimneys.

Number Series: 30900 to 30939.

Historical Notes: The famous "Schools" class which was designed to replace the "L" class on trains of increasing weight. These are the heaviest 4–4–0 type locomotives in Great Britain, and have been claimed as the most powerful of that type in Europe.

Location: Until recently confined entirely to express passenger trains on the South Eastern section. A number of them have since been displaced by multiple unit Diesel trains on the Hastings line and have been drafted to the South Western section of the S.R.

30950–30957

Origin: Southern Railway.
Introduced: March, 1929.
Driving Wheel: 4 ft. 8 in.
Length: 39 ft. 4 in.
Weight: 71 tons 12 cwt.
Water Capacity: 1,500 gals.
Designer: R. E. L. Maunsell.

Purpose: Heavy Shunting Duties.
Cylinders (3): 16 in. × 18 in.
Boiler Pressure: 180 lb.sq.in.
Tractive Effort: 29,376 lb.
Coal Capacity: 3 tons.
Power Classification: 6–F.

Additional Identification Features: Footplate raised over cylinders and dropped under bunker. Outside cylinders with Walschaert's valve-gear. Short side-tanks with sloping top towards front end. Deep buffer-beam. Smoke-box of smaller diameter than boiler-cleading. Twin Ross "Pop" safety-valves on round-topped fire-box.

Number Series: 30950 to 30957.

Historical Notes: A very powerful class designed primarily for heavy shunting work: the eight engines comprising the class were built at Brighton works.

Location: All at Exmouth Junction.

31004–31725

Origin: S. E. & C. R.
Introduced: June, 1900.
Driving Wheel: 5 ft. 2 in.
Weight: (Engine) 43 tons 16 cwt.
Water Capacity: 3,300 gals.

Designer: Harry Wainwright.
Purpose: Freight.
Cylinders (2): 18½ in. × 26 in.
Boiler Pressure: 160 lb. sq. in.
Tractive Effort: 19,520 lb.
Power Classification: 2–F.

Additional Identification Features: Twin safety-valves mounted on flat-topped saddle on round-topped fire-box.

Number Series: 31004, 31037, 31054, 31061, 31068, 31086, 31102, 31112–13, 31150, 31218, 31223, 31229, 31242, 31244, 31255–6, 31267–8, 31271, 31280, 31287, 31293, 31298, 31317, 31480–1, 31495, 31498, 31510, 31573, 31575, 31578–9, 31583, 31584, 31588–89–90, 31592, 31682/4/6/9, 31690/1/3–5, 31714–7/9, 31720–5.

Historical Notes: 109 engines of this class were built between 1900 and 1908. No. 31685 was rebuilt as a saddle-tank in 1917, for shunting at Bricklayers Arms, but is now scrapped.

Location: To be seen all over the lines of the former S.E. & C.R. Mainly general purpose freight engines, but used on all kinds of duties, including local passenger on which they are still sometimes to be seen.

0-4-4T

31005–31554

Origin: S. E. & C. R.
Introduced: 1904.
Driving Wheel: 5 ft. 6 in.
Trailing Wheel: 3 ft. 7 in.
Length: 33 ft.
Weight: 54 tons 8 cwt.
Water Capacity: 1,150 to 1,350 gals.

Designer: Harry Wainwright.
Purpose: (Originally) Suburban Passenger.
Cylinders (2): 18 in. × 26 in.
Boiler Pressure: 160 lb. sq. in.
Tractive Effort: 17,360 lb.
Coal Capacity: 2 tons 5 cwt.
Power Classification: 1-P.

Additional Identification Features: "Pagoda" cab; roof overhangs characteristically on each side of cab. On some engines top of bunker flared outwards. Twin safety-valves mounted on flat-topped base.

Number Series: 31005, 31161/2/77/93, 31261/3/5/6, 31276/8, 31305–8/10, 31322/4/6/8, 31500/12, 31517–22, 31530/3, 31542–4, 31550–3.

Historical Notes: Originally designed to replace the hitherto standard S.E. & C.R. "Q" class passenger tanks and to cope with the continually increasing suburban passenger traffic in the days before electrification.

Location: Many are now fitted for pull and push working, and are mainly found in the country areas of Kent, Surrey and Sussex. Others are used on empty carriage workings, in the London area.

"D-1" and "E-1" CLASSES 4-4-0

31019–31749

Origin: S.E. and C.R.
Introduced: May, 1921.
Driving Wheel: 6 ft. 8 in.
Bogie Wheel: 3 ft. 7 in.
Length: 54 ft. 11¾ in.
Weight: 91 tons 4 cwt.
Water Capacity: 3,300 gals.
Designer: R. E. L. Maunsell (rebuild).

Purpose: Express Passenger (Chatham Section).
Cylinders (2): 19 in. × 26 in.
Boiler Pressure: 180 lb. sq. in.
Tractive Effort: 17,950 lb.
Coal Capacity: 4 tons 10 cwt.
Power Classification: 3–P.

Additional Identification Features: Inside cylinders. Footplate sharply upswept to a higher level over driving wheels.

Number Series: 31145, 31246–7, 31487, 31489, 31494, 31505, 31509, 31545, 31727, 31735, 31739, and 31749 (class D1).   31019, 31067, 31497, 31507 (class E1).

Historical Notes: Rebuilds of Wainwright's un-superheated class D and E engines into virtually one class with only very minor differences.

Location: Now employed chiefly on secondary and stopping passenger trains on the South Eastern section, but still occasionally used on express services.

"P" CLASS

0-6-0T

31027, 31323, 31556

Origin: S.E. & C.R.
Introduced: Feb., 1909.
Driving Wheel: 3 ft. 9¼ in.
Length: 24 ft. 1⅜ in.
Weight: 28 tons 10 cwt.
Water Capacity: 550 gals.
Designer: Harry Wainwright.

Purpose: Light Shunting Duties.
Cylinders (2): 12 in. × 18 in.
Boiler Pressure: 160 lb. sq. in.
Tractive Effort: 7,810 lb.
Coal Capacity: 18 cwt.
Power Classification: Unclassed.

Additional Identification Features: Noticeably a very small engine with tall, narrow chimney, normal dome and twin safety-valves mounted on a flat saddle immediately in front of cab. Tanks square. Overhanging roof "Pagoda" cab. Very small splashers to leading wheels.

Number Series: 31027, 31323, 31556.

Historical Notes: Primarily designed for working light branch services and rail motor ("push-pull") sets, principally between Nunhead Junction and Greenwich Park, Otford and Sevenoaks, and Reading and Ash. It was found that the engines were too small for such work, and they were distributed over the system to work on light shunting duties and as shed pilots.

Location: Two at Folkestone and one at Brighton.

31048, 31065, 31258

Origin: South Eastern Railway.
Introduced: 1878.
Designer: J. Stirling.
Purpose: Freight.

Driving Wheel: 5 ft. 2 in.
Cylinders (2): 18 in × 26 in.
Boiler Pressure: 150 lb. sq. in.
Tractive Effort: 17,325 lb.

Additional Identification Features: Distinguished from "C" class (page 81) by longer chimney and tender with springs above the footplate.

Number Series: 31048, 31065, 31258.

Historical Notes: Rebuilds by Wainwright or Stirling engine originally with domeless boiler. Three survivors of a once numerous class.

Location: Stationed at Dover for working coal traffic on the remaining portion of the East Kent Railway.

31610–31639, 31790–31809

Origin: S. E. & C. R.
Introduced: June, 1928.
Driving Wheel: 6 ft.
Pony Wheel: 3 ft. 1 in.
Length: 57 ft. 9⅞ in.
Weight: 110 tons 14 cwt.(appr.).
Water Capacity: 4,000 gals.

Designer: R. E. L. Maunsell.
Purpose: Mixed Traffic.
Cylinders (2): 19 in. × 28 in.
Boiler Pressure: 200 lb. sq. in.
Tractive Effort: 23,866 lb.
Coal Capacity: 5 tons.
Power Classification: 4-P/3-F.

Additional Identification Features: The majority of the 31790–31809 have flat-sided tenders, the others as shown in the illustration.

Number Series: 31790 to 31809 (rebuilt "Rivers"); 31610 to 31639 (newly-built engines).

Historical Notes: Originally this class was one of rebuilds from the old S.E. & C.R. "River" or "K" class, 2-6-4T. Nos. 31610 to 31639 (the first ten commenced as tanks, but altered before completion) were also built to the same design, but with smaller splashers and minor differences from the rebuilt "Rivers". The original, No. 31790, was built by the S.E. & C.R. in 1917. Nos. 31791–31809 were added by the S.R. 1925–6.

Location: Most of the class are to be seen on miscellaneous passenger work on the South Eastern and Brighton sections, but there are also several around Eastleigh and Bournemouth, and a number at Yeovil.

31753–31759, 31782–31789

Origin: Southern Railway.
Introduced: March, 1926.
Driving Wheel: 6 ft. 8 in.
Bogie Wheel: 3 ft. 7 in.
Length: 56 ft. 7⅞ in.
Weight: 98 tons 8 cwt.
Water Capacity: 3,500 gals.
Designer: R. E. L. Maunsell.

Purpose: Passenger.
Cylinders (2): 19½ in. × 26 in.
Boiler Pressure: 180 lb.sq.in.
Tractive Effort: 18,910 lb.
Coal Capacity: 5 tons.
Power Classification: 3–P.

Additional Identification Features: A somewhat larger engine than the rather similar "D-1" and "E-1" classes (see page 83), and easily distinguished from them by the flat-sided tender.

Number Series: 31753 to 31759, 31782 to 31789, with gaps due to scrapping.

Historical Notes: A post-grouping development of the "L" class (*q.v.*) with long-travel valves, cab side-window and other minor alterations. Built by the North British Locomotive Co., Ltd. in Glasgow.

Location: Mostly to be found on the lines of the former S.E. & C.R.

"L" CLASS

31760–31781

Origin: S.E. & C.R.
Introduced: July, 1914.
Driving Wheel: 6 ft. 8 in.
Bogie Wheel: 3 ft. 7 in.
Length: 56 ft. 7⅞ in.
Weight: 98 tons 6 cwt.
Water Capacity: 3,500 gals.
Designer: Harry Wainwright.

Purpose: Express Passenger.
Cylinders (2): 19½ in. × 26 in.
Boiler Pressure: 180 lb.sq.in.
Coal Capacity: 5 tons.
Tractive Effort: 18,910 lb.
Power Classification: 3-P.

Additional Identification Features: Front splasher complete, but rear one merging into front of cab. No cab side-windows. Square-topped Belpaire fire-box with two Ross "Pop" safety-valves on top. Straight running-plate and wide splashers (distinction from "L-1" class).

Number Series: 31760 to 31781, with gaps due to scrapping.

Historical Notes: A development of the "D" class; Wainwright had left the S.E. & C.R. before delivery commenced, and Maunsell made a few alterations, such as substituting black beading for the brass on the splasher rims. Ten engines of the class were built in Germany by Messrs. Borsig, and were consequently nicknamed "Germans". Twelve more were built by Messrs. Beyer-Peacock in Manchester.

Location: All the survivors are now allocated to Nine Elms.

31400–31414, 31810–31875

Origin: S.E. & C.R.
Introduced: ("N") Aug., 1917.
Driving Wheel: 5 ft. 6 in.
Pony Wheel: 3 ft. 1 in.
Length: 57 ft. 9⅝ in.
Weight: 61 tons 4 cwt.
Water Capacity: 4,000 gals.

Designer: R. E. L. Maunsell.
Purpose: Mixed Traffic.
Cylinders (2): 19 in. × 28 in.
Boiler Pressure: 200 lb. sq. in.
Tractive Effort: 26,035 lb.
Coal Capacity: 5 tons.
Power Classification: 4–P/5–F.

Additional Identification Features: Footplate straight from front of cylinder to centre-line of cab, where it drops to buffer-beam level.

Number Series: 31400 to 31414, 31810 to 31821, 31823 to 31875.

Historical Notes: Engine Nos. 31826 to 31875 were built at Woolwich Arsenal during the years 1924–25, the balance were built at Ashford.

Location: To be found on the South Eastern and Brighton sections and also in considerable numbers in the West of England, mainly west of Exeter.

31822, 31876–31880

Origin: S.E. & C.R.
Designer: R. E. L. Maunsell.
Introduced: 1922.
Purpose: Freight.

Driving Wheel: 5 ft. 6 in.
Cylinders (3): 16 in. × 28 in.
Boiler Pressure: 200 lb. sq. in.
Tractive Effort: 27,695 lb.

Additional Identification Features: Distinguished from class "N" by smaller cylinders.

Number Series: 31822, 31876–31880.

Historical Notes: The five later engines were built in 1930, and were primarily intended for working over the Tonbridge–Hastings road, which has narrower clearance restrictions, prohibiting the use of many classes of engine. The use of three smaller cylinders in place of two longer ones enabled the overall width to be reduced sufficiently to permit their working on this line.

Location: All now stationed at Hither Green.

31890–31910

Origin: Southern Railway.
•Introduced: 1928.
Driving Wheel: 6 ft.
Pony Wheel: 3 ft. 1 in.
Length: 57 ft. 9½ in.
Total Weight: 107 tons 14 cwt.
Water Capacity: 4,000 gals.

Designer: R. E. L. Maunsell.
Purpose: Mixed Traffic.
Cylinders (3): 16 in. × 28 in.
Boiler Pressure: 200 lb. sq. in.
Tractive Effort: 25,387 lb.
Coal Capacity: 5 tons.
Power Classification: 4–P/3–F.

Additional Identification Features: Footplate almost level from front buffer-beam to centre-line of cab side. Cylinders have sloping sides and appear more set back under footplating than on "U" class engines. (See also "U" and "N" classes.) No. 31890 has footplate raised over cylinders, then dropped slightly over coupled wheels, bigger splashers and more rounded cab corners; originally a 2–6–4T ("River Frome").

Number Series: 31890 to 31910.

Historical Notes: Development of "U" class (*q.v.*) which were also rebuilt from S.E. and C.R. "K" class ("Rivers"), which were 2–6–4 tanks. Three cylinders were provided on the "U–1's" instead of two used on "U" class.

Location: Nearly all on the South Eastern section.

• The new engines were built in 1931 at Eastleigh.

"W" CLASS

2-6-4T

31911–31925

Origin: Southern Railway.
Introduced: Dec., 1931.
Driving Wheel: 5 ft. 6 in.
Pony Wheel: 3 ft. 1 in.
Trailing Wheel: 3 ft. 1 in.
Length: 44 ft. ¼ in.
Weight: 90 tons 14 cwt.
Water Capacity: 2,000 gals.
Designer: R. E. L. Maunsell.

Purpose: Mixed Traffic.
Cylinders (3): 16½ in. × 28 in.
Boiler Pressure: 200 lb.sq.in.
Tractive Effort: 29,452 lb.
Coal Capacity: 3 tons 10 cwt.
Power Classification: 6–F.

Additional Identification Features: Easily recognised by cut-out in tanks to clear valve-gear.   Distinctive steps over valve gear, to running plate.

Number Series: 31911 to 31925.

Historical Notes: Developed by Mr. Maunsell from his 1922 "N–1" class, which were themselves a development of the 1917 "N" class of the old South Eastern and Chatham Railway.

Location: Used entirely on transfer freight traffic between North and South London, from Willesden via the West London line to Hither Green, Norwood Junction, etc.

32100–32109

Origin: L.B.S.C.R.
*Introduced: May, 1913.
Driving Wheel: 4 ft. 6 in.
†Weight: 52 tons 15 cwt.
Designer: L. B. Billinton.
Purpose: Local Freight Work and Shunting.

Cylinders (2): 17½ in. × 26 in.
Boiler Pressure: 170 lb.sq.in.
Tractive Effort: 21,305 lb.
Power Classification: 3–F.

Additional Identification Features: Raised footplate upswept at front and rear. Normal chimney and dome, with waisted safety-valve casing mounted on round-topped fire-box. Nos. 32105 to 32109 have tanks cut away at lower front end to give side access to motion.

Number Series: 32100 to 32109.

Historical Notes: These engines replaced some of the earlier "E-1" class which were scrapped in 1913. There are two varieties, viz., the later five (Nos. 32105 to 32109) having the top of the tanks extended further forward, and the earlier five (Nos. 32100 to 32104) with shorter tanks. (See footnote below.)

Location: Stewarts Lane (4), Norwood Junction (2), Southampton Docks (4).

* Nos. 32105 to 32109 built 1915–16.
† Nos. 32105 to 32109, 53 tons 10 cwt.

"K" CLASS

2-6-0

32337–32353

Origin: L.B.S.C.R.
Introduced: Sept., 1913.
Driving Wheel: 5 ft. 6 in.
Pony Wheel: 3 ft. 6 in.
Length: 57 ft. 10 in.
Total Weight: 105 tons 5 cwt.
Water Capacity: 3,940 gals.

Designer: L. B. Billinton.
Purpose: Mixed Traffic.
Cylinders (2): 21 in. × 26 in.
Boiler Pressure: 170 lb.sq.in.
Tractive Effort: 25,100 lb.
Coal Capacity: 4 tons.
Power Classification: 4–P/5–F.

Additional Identification Features: Footplate raised over driving-wheels with double curve. Outside cylinders but inside valve-gear. Flat-topped dome and safety-valve connected by lever to cab. Splashers independent, rear one being merged with cab front.

Number Series: 32337 to 32353.

Historical Notes: These "Mogul" engines were at one time used on the heaviest goods trains on the L.B.S.C.R., and were then shedded at Brighton, Fratton and Norwood. A Class "M" 2–6–2T based on these engines was contemplated in 1916, but the Government requested more "K" class (342 to 346).

Location: All still at work on the Brighton section.

"E-6" CLASS   0-6-2T

32407–32418

Origin: L.B.S.C.R.
Introduced: ("E-6") Dec., 1904. ("E-6x" rebuilds of class "E-6") July, 1911.
Driving Wheel: 4 ft. 6 in.
Trailing Wheel: 4 ft.
Weight: ("E-6") 61 tons. ("E-6x") 63 tons.
Designer: R. J. Billinton.

Purpose: Light Local Freight and Shunting.
Cylinders: 18 in × 26 in.
Boiler Pressure: 160–175 lb. sq. in.
Tractive Effort: ("E-6") 21,215 lb. ("E-6x") 23,000 lb. (approx.).
Power Classification: 3-F.

Number Series: 32407–32418, of which only Nos. 32408, 32410, and 32415–8 now survive.

Location: Divided between Bricklayers Arms and Dover.

32438–32451, 32521–32553

Origin: L.B.S.C.R.
Introduced: July, 1908.
Driving Wheel: 5 ft.
Weight: (Engine) 45 tons 5 cwt.
Designer: D. Earle Marsh.

Purpose: Freight.
Cylinders (2): 17½ in. × 26 in.
Boiler Pressure: 170 lb.sq.in.
Tractive Effort: 19,175 lb.
Power Classification: 2–F.

Additional Identification Features: Some engines have two domes of identical size and shape fitted, the one next the chimney was in connection with feed water heating and is now blanked off.

Number Series: The class originally ran from 32433–32452 and 32521–32555, of which Nos. 32438, 32441/3/5/6/8–51, 32521–3/5/7/8, 32532/4–6/8/9, and 32541/3–50/2/3 now survive.

Historical Notes: Rebuilds of R. J. Billinton's earlier "C–2" class engines, with 5 ft. diameter boilers and extended smoke-boxes.

Location: All still at work on the Brighton section.

32468–32515, 32556–32581

Origin: L.B.S.C.R.
Introduced: 1897.
Driving Wheel: 5 ft.
Weight: 58 tons (approx.).
Designer: R. J. Billinton.
Purpose: Suburban Mixed Traffic.

Cylinders: $17\frac{1}{2}$ in. × 26 in.
Boiler Pressure: 170 lb.sq.in.
Tractive Effort: 19,175 lb.
Power Classification: 2–P/ 2–F.

Number Series: 32468–70/2–5/9, 32484/7, 32491/5/8, 32500/3–6/9, 32510/2/5, 32556/7/9, 32562–5, 32578, 32580/1. The class originally ran from 32463–32520 and 32556–32582.

Historical Notes: Built in considerable numbers for London suburban passenger working. Many were sent to county districts on electrification, and latterly the survivors have been mainly engaged on shunting.

Location: Mostly still on the Brighton section, but there are some at Eastleigh and a few on empty carriage workings between Clapham Junction and Waterloo.

DS 680, 681, 32635–32678

Origin: L.B.S.C.R.
Introduced: Oct., 1872.
Driving Wheel: 4 ft.
Length: 26 ft. ½ in.
Weight: 28 tons 5 cwt.
Water Capacity: 500 gals.
Designer: William Stroudley.

Purpose: Light Passenger and Shunting.
Cylinders (2): 12 in. × 20 in.
Boiler Pressure: 150 lb. sq. in.
Tractive Effort: 10,695 lb.
Coal Capacity: 1 ton.
Power Classification: 0–P.

Additional Identification Features: An extremely small locomotive with very tall, narrow chimney, dome with Salter valves.

Number Series: 32635/6, 32640/6, 32650, 32661/2, 32670/8. (Also service locos. No. DS 680, and DS 681 not included in capital stock total.)

Historical Features: A very famous class of extremely powerful engines for their diminutive size. Nos. 32636 and 32670 are now the oldest engines in service on British Railways.

Location: Most of the survivors are retained for working the Hayling Island branch; others are stationed at Brighton. DS 680/1 are at Lancing carriage works.

* Engine No. 32636: 14$\frac{3}{16}$ in. × 20 in.

"E-1" CLASS 0-6-0T

4, 32694

Origin: L.B.S.C.R.
Introduced: Nov., 1874.
Driving Wheel: 4 ft. 6 in.
Length: 32 ft. 4¼ in.
Weight: 44 tons 3 cwt.
Water Capacity: 900 gals.
Designer: William Stroudley.

Purpose: Light General Work.
Cylinders (2): 17 in. × 24 in.
Boiler Pressure: 160 lb.sq.in.
Tractive Effort: 17,500 lb.
Coal Capacity: 1 ton 10 cwt.
Power Classification: 2–F.

Additional Identification Features: A larger version of "A–1" class (*q.v.*). Straight footplate. Rounded top edge to side-tanks. Cab roof bulges upward to its centre.

Number Series: 32694. Also (on Isle of Wight) W–4.

Historical Notes: This was Mr. Stroudley's first type of goods tank engine, of which no less than 72 were built between 1874 and 1883 at Brighton works, and of which there remain but two survivors.

Location: Southampton Docks (No. 32694), Isle of Wight (No. 4).

"Q-1" CLASS

33001–33040

Origin: Southern Railway.
Introduced: March, 1942.
Driving Wheel: 5 ft. 1 in.
Length: 54 ft. 10½ in.
Total Weight: 89 tons 5 cwt.
Water Capacity: 3,700 gals.
Designer: O. V. Bulleid.

Purpose: Freight
Cylinders: (2): 19 in. × 26 in.
Boiler Pressure: 230 lb. sq. in.
Tractive Effort: 30,080 lb.
Coal Capacity: 5 tons.
Power Classification: 5–F.

Additional Identification Features: This Southern class is the most unusual class ever to be designed in this country. It is devoid of a footplate and wheel splashers. The cast wheels are not spoked, but have holes and recesses in their discs. (See "Merchant Navy", "Battle of Britain", and "West Country" classes.) The outside cleading of the boiler casing is not cylindrical, and is in three sections, of which the smoke-box end is of a similar shape to a tunnel mouth. Large, squat chimney and flat-topped "dome".

Number Series: 33001 to 33040.

Historical Notes: This unconventional class immediately attracted attention when it was introduced during the Second World War as an "Austerity" design giving maximum tractive effort with minimum weight per axle. An exceedingly serviceable type which eliminated "double-heading" during the war days on secondary lines.

Location: To be seen on most parts of the Southern system within about 75 miles of London, but rarely in the West of England.

"WEST COUNTRY" CLASS 4-6-2

34001–34110

Origin: Southern Railway.
Introduced: May, 1945.
Driving Wheel: 6 ft. 2 in.
Bogie Wheel: 3 ft. 1 in.
Trailing Wheel: 3 ft. 1 in.
Length: 67 ft. 4¼ in.
Total Weight: 128 tons 12 cwt.
Water Capacity: 4,500 gals.

Designer: O. V. Bulleid.
Purpose: Express Passenger.
Cylinders (3): 16¾ in. × 24 in.
Boiler Pressure: 250 lb. sq. in.
Tractive Effort: 27,720 lb.
Coal Capacity: 5 tons.
Power Classification: 7-P 5-F.

Additional Identification Features: Engine nearly 2 ft. shorter than "Merchant Navy" class. Trailing wheels 6 in. smaller in diameter than the tender wheels, "Merchant Navy" class being of same size; though this is hardly noticeable. Top of tender sides not turned inwards. Cylinder casing does not extend to front buffer-beam. Many of the class are now having the streamlined casing removed and are being otherwise rebuilt, so that they now closely resemble the altered "Merchant Navies" as illustrated on the next page.

Number series: 34001 to 34110.

Historical Notes Designed as a smaller version of the "Merchant Navy" class bearing only 18¼ tons on each driving axle, which enables "West Country" engines to be used with safety almost anywhere on the Region from Padstow to Dover.

Location: Seen on express passenger duties on all the principal non-electrified main lines of the Southern Railway.

"MERCHANT NAVY" CLASS 4-6-2

35001–35030

Origin: Southern Railway.
Introduced: June, 1941.
Driving Wheel: 6 ft. 2 in.
Bogie Wheel: 3 ft. 1 in.
Trailing Wheel: 3 ft. 7 in.
Length: 69 ft. 7¾ in.
*Weight: (without tender) 94 tons 15 cwt.

Water Capacity: 5,000 gals.
Designer: O. V. Bulleid.
Purpose: Express Passenger.
Cylinders (3): 18 in. × 24 in.
Boiler Pressure: 250 lb.sq.in.
Tractive Effort: 33,493 lb.
Coal Capacity: 5 tons.
Power Classification: 8–P.

Additional Identification Features: These engines were built with streamlined casing, resembling the "West Country" class as illustrated on the preceding page. All have, however, been rebuilt as illustrated above.

Number Series: 35001 to 35030.

Historical Notes: Produced by Bulleid when he joined the Southern Railway from Doncaster, where he had been assistant to Sir Nigel Gresley of the L.N.E.R. An engine full of original ideas, such as chain-driven valve-gear.

Location: Confined to the main lines between Waterloo and Weymouth and Waterloo and Exeter.

* Weight increased to 97 tons 18 cwt. in the rebuilt engines.

FOWLER 3-MT CLASS   2–6–2T

40001–40070

Origin: L.M.S.
Introduced: March, 1930.
Driving Wheel: 5 ft. 3 in.
Pony Wheel: 3 ft. 3½ in.
Trailing Wheel: 3 ft. 3½ in.
Length: 41 ft. 11¾ in.
Weight: 70 tons 10 cwt.
Water Capacity: 1,500 gals.
Designer: Sir Henry Fowler.

*Purpose: Suburban Passenger.
Cylinders (2): 17½ in. × 26 in.
Boiler Pressure: 200 lb.sq.in.
Tractive Effort: 21,485 lb.
Coal Capacity: 3 tons.
Power Classification: 3–MT.

Additional Identification Features: Most easily identified by Number Series (*q.v.*). Identifiable from other L.M. Region 2–6–2T's by its parallel boiler, and smoke-box curving down to meet the frames.

Number Series: 40001 to 40070, with gaps due to scrapping.

Location: Found on the former L.M.S. section.

* Some engines (Nos. 40021 to 40040) were fitted with condensing apparatus for working through the tunnels to Moorgate Street, London, in which case their weight was increased to 71 tons 16 cwt. A few are motor fitted for pull and push working.

"STANIER 3-MT" CLASS 2-6-2T

40071–40209

Origin: L.M.S.
Introduced: Feb., 1935.
Driving Wheel: 5 ft. 3 in.
Pony Wheel: 3 ft. 3½ in.
Trailing Wheel: 3 ft. 3½ in.
Length: 41 ft. 11¾ in.
Weight: 71 tons 5 cwt.
Water Capacity: 1,500 gals.

Designer: Sir William Stanier.
Purpose: Mixed Traffic.
Cylinders (2): 17½ in. × 26 in.
Boiler Pressure: 200 lb.sq.in.
Tractive Effort: 21,485 lb.
Coal Capacity: 3 tons.
Power Classification: 3–MT.

Additional Identification Features: Similar to Fowler 2-6-2T (40001), but with pronounced slope to top of side-tanks, and taper boilers.

Number Series: 40071 to 40209, with gaps due to scrapping.

Historical Notes: A development of the 1930 Fowler 2-6-2T's (p. 103) of which four engines (Nos. 40148, 40163, 40169 and 40203) were fitted in 1941 with larger boilers, resulting in increased weight of 72 tons 10 cwt.

Location: Widely scattered over the Midland Region, with a few on the Western and North Eastern (Leeds area), and a number in Scotland, mainly around Glasgow.

40396–40557

Origin: Midland Railway.
Introduced: 1912.
Driving Wheel: 7 ft. 0½ in.
Designer: R. M. Deeley.
Purpose: Express Passenger.

Cylinders: 20½ in. × 26 in.
Boiler Pressure: 160 lb. sq. in.
Tractive Effort: 17,585 lb.
Power Classification: 2–P.

Additional Identification Features: Until recently fitted with earlier Midland type tender with coal rails. Some of the survivors have acquired flat-sided tenders as fitted to the L.M.S. development of the class (see next page).

Number Series: 40396, 40402, 40411, 40421, 40439, 40443, 40452–4, 40487/9, 40491, 40501/2/4, 40511, 40537, 40540/3/8, 40552/7.

Historical Notes: Survivors of a once numerous class of engine rebuilt by Deeley from 1912 onwards, originally constructed by Johnson between 1882 and 1901.

Location: Scattered amongst various sheds of the former M.R. system, chiefly in the Midlands.

40563–40700

Origin: L.M.S.
Introduced: 1928.
Driving Wheel: 6 ft. 9 in.
Designer: Sir Henry Fowler.
Purpose: Express Passenger.

Cylinders: 19 in. × 26 in.
Boiler Pressure: 180 lb. sq. in.
Tractive Effort: 17,730 lb.
Power Classification: 2–P.

Number Series: 40563–40700, with gaps due to scrapping.

Historical Notes: Development of the M.R. Deeley rebuilds (see previous page) adopted by the L.M.S.R. as a standard light passenger engine.

Location: Found scattered over most parts of the former L.M.S. system. A number are in Scotland, principally in the area around Kilmarnock.

6 ft. 9 in. "COMPOUND" CLASS 4-4-0

40900–41199

Origin: L.M.S.
Introduced: 1924.
Driving Wheel: 6 ft. 9 in.
Weight: (Engine) 61 tons 14 cwt.
Designers: Johnson & Deeley.
Purpose: Passenger Express.

Cylinders: High Pressure: (1) 19 in. × 26 in. Low Pressure: (2) 21 in. × 26 in.
Boiler Pressure: 200 lb.sq.in.
Tractive Effort: 22,650 lb.
Power Classification: 4–P.

Number Series: The class originally ran from 40900–40939 and 41045–41199, but in August 1960 only Nos. 40907, 40936, 41063 and 41168 remained in stock.

Historical Notes: A development of the Johnson Midland 7 ft. "Compound" with modifications. This once popular and highly efficient class performed splendid work during the earlier years of the grouping not only on its native Midland system, but on the main lines of the C.R. and G. & S.W.R. in Scotland and on the Birmingham two-hour expresses from Euston.

Location: No. 40907 at Millhouses (Sheffield), 41063 at Bradford and the other two at Monument Lane (Birmingham).

IVATT 2-MT CLASS

2-6-2T

41200–41329

Origin: L.M.S.
Introduced: 1946.
Driving Wheel: 5 ft.
Pony Wheel: 3 ft.
Trailing Wheel: 3 ft.
Length: 38 ft. 9½ in.
Weight: 63 tons 5 cwt.
Water Capacity: 1,350 gals.

Designer: H. G. Ivatt.
Purpose: Suburban Passenger.
*Cylinders (2): 16 in. × 24 in.
Boiler Pressure: 200 lb. sq. in.
**Tractive Effort:* 17,410 lb.
Coal Capacity: 3 tons.
Power Classification: 2–MT.
(2–PT/2–FT on S.R.).

Additional Identification Features: Footplate raised over cylinders and motion with break in front of cylinders. Small boiler. Bunker tapered towards top. Cab doors cut into cab roof. Sloping steam pipes from above cylinders to smoke-box sides. Mechanical lubricators in front of steam pipes. (Compare B.R. class—page 232).

Number Series: 41200 to 41289 (16 in. × 24 in. cylinders, 17,410 lb. tractive effort), 41290 to 41329 (16½ in. × 24 in. cylinders, 18,510 lb. tractive effort).

Location: The majority are widely scattered over the L.M. Region, many motor-fitted for pull and push working. A number are in the North Eastern Region, whilst 41290–41319 are on the Southern, some in the London area and others at Eastleigh and in the West of England.

"DEELEY DOCK TANK" CLASS 0–4–0T

41528–41537

Origin: Midland Railway.
Introduced: 1907.
Designer: R. M. Deeley.
Purpose: Dock shunting, etc.

Driving Wheel: 3 ft. 9¾ in.
Cylinders (2): 15 in. × 22 in.
Boiler Pressure: 160 lb.sq.in.
Tractive Effort: 14,635 lb.

Additional Identification Features: Long side tanks extending full length of boiler, Walschaerts valve-gear.

Number Series: 41528, 41529, 41531–41533, 41535–41537.

Historical Notes: Constructed for shunting at docks and collieries over lines of sharp curvature.

Location: Four at Staveley, two at Burton and two at Gloucester.

41702–41885

Origin: Midland Railway.
Introduced: 1878.
Driving Wheel: 4 ft. 7 in.
Weight: 39 tons 11 cwt.
Designer: S. W. Johnson.
Purpose: Freight and Shunt-
ing.

Cylinders (2): 17 in. × 24 in.
Boiler Pressure: 140/150 lb.
sq. in.
Tractive Effort: 15,005/
16,080 lb.
Power Classification: 1–F.

Additional Identification Features: Some engines are
devoid of any back sheet to the cab, having only a weather-
board and short roof. No. 41835 still carries the Johnson
boiler with Salter safety-valves on the dome.

Number Series: 41702/8, 41712, 41734/9, 41763/9, 41773,
41804, 41835, 41844, 41875.

Historical Notes: Survivors of a large class built between
1878 and 1899.

Location: The 12 remaining engines of this class are found
at various sheds of the former Midland Railway, six of them
being at Staveley.

STANIER "PUSH-PULL" TANK　　　0—4—4T

41900

Origin: L.M.S.
Introduced: Nov., 1932.
Driving Wheel: 5 ft. 7 in.
Weight: 58 tons 1 cwt.
Designer: Sir William Stanier.

Purpose: Passenger "Push-pull".
Cylinders: 18 in. × 26 in.
Boiler Pressure: 160 lb.sq.in.
Tractive Effort: 17,100 lb.
Power Classification: 2–P.

Number Series: 41900 to 41909. All except No. 41900 are now withdrawn.

Historical Notes: One of Sir William Stanier's first designs for the L.M.S.

Location: The last survivor is allocated to the Gloucester district for work on the Tewkesbury branch.

41947

Origin: London, Tilbury and Southend Railway.
Introduced: 1923.
Driving Wheel: 6 ft. 6 in.
Bogie Wheel: 3 ft. 2 in.
Weight: 71 tons 10 cwt.

Designer: Thomas Whitelegg.
Purpose: Passenger.
Cylinders (2): 19 in. × 26 in.
Boiler Pressure: 170 lb. sq. in.
Tractive Effort: 17,390 lb.
Power Classification: 3–P.

Number Series: 41928 to 41978, of which only No. 41947 remains.

Historical Notes: L.M.S. development of L.T. & S.R. design of 1905, built between 1923 and 1930.

Location: Allocated to Toton.

41981

Origin: L.T. and S.R.
Introduced: 1903.
Driving Wheel: 5 ft. 3 in.
Weight: 64 tons 13 cwt.
Designer: Thomas White-
legg.

Purpose: Local Freight.
Cylinders: 18 in. × 26 in.
Boiler Pressure: 170 lb.sq.in.
Tractive Effort: 19,320 lb.
Power Classification: 3–F.

Number Series: 41980 to 41993, of which only No. 41981 remains.

Historical Notes: Engine Nos. 41990–1–2–3 were built in 1912 and taken into Midland Railway stock in that year. The other previously ran on L.T. & S.R. Nos. 69–78.

Location: Allocated to Tilbury.

STANIER AND FAIRBURN 4–MT CLASS 2–6–4T

42050–42299, 42425–42494, 42537–42699

Origin: L.M.S.
Introduced: March, 1945.
Driving Wheel: 5 ft. 9 in.
Pony Wheel: 3 ft. 3½ in.
Trailing Wheel: 3 ft. 3½ in.
Length: 45 ft. 9¾ in.
Weight: 85 tons 5 cwt.
Water Capacity: 2,000 gals.

Designers: Stanier and Fairburn.
Purpose: Suburban Passenger.
Cylinders (2): 19⅝ in. × 26 in.
Boiler Pressure: 200 lb. sq. in.
Tractive Effort: 24,670 lb.
Coal Capacity: 3 tons 10 cwt.
Power Classification: 4–MT. (4–PT/4–FT on S. Region.)

Additional Identification Features: The Stanier engines are most easily distinguished by not having the gap in the running plate ahead of the cylinder, which is found in the Fairburn engines.

Number Series: Stanier engines, 42425–42494, 42537–42672. One or two of the Stanier engines have recently been scrapped. Fairburn engines, 42050–42299, 42673–42699.

Historical Notes: Later developments of original Fowler 2–6–4T's of 1927. The class is also perpetuated with slight modifications as a B.R. standard design (80000 class).

Location: Found widely scattered in all Regions except the Western and the Southern.

FOWLER 4–MT CLASS

42300–42424

Origin: L.M.S.
Introduced: Dec., 1927.
Driving Wheel: 5 ft. 9 in.
Pony Wheel: 3 ft. 3½ in.
Trailing Wheel: 3 ft. 3½ in.
Length: 47 ft. 2¼ in.
Weight: 86 tons 5 cwt.
Water Capacity: 2,000 gals.
Designer: Sir Henry Fowler.

Purpose: Suburban Passenger.
Cylinders (2): 19 in. × 26 in.
Boiler Pressure: 200 lb.sq.in.
Tractive Effort: 23,125 lb.
Coal Capacity: 3 tons 10 cwt.
Power Classification: 4–MT.

Additional Identification Features: Parallel boiler, as distinct from the taper boilers in the later Stanier and Fairburn engines (see previous page). Nos. 42395 onwards have side windows to cabs.

Number Series: 42300 to 42394 (introduced 1927); 42395 to 42424 (introduced 1933), with gaps due to scrapping.

Location: Mostly at various sheds on the L.M. Region, with some on the N.E. and a few on what is now the Western Region (but was formerly L.N.W.R.) working between Shrewsbury and Swansea.

STANIER 3-CYLINDER 4–MT CLASS   2–6–4T

42500–42536

Origin: L.M.S.
Introduced: June, 1934.
Driving Wheel: 5 ft. 9 in.
Pony Wheel: 3 ft. 3½ in.
Trailing Wheel: 3 ft. 3½ in.
Length: 47 ft. 2¾ in.
Weight: 92 tons 5 cwt.
Water Capacity: 2,000 gals.
Designer: Sir   William
Stanier.

Purpose: Suburban Passenger.
Cylinders (3): 16 in. × 26 in.
Boiler Pressure: 200 lb.sq.in.
Tractive Effort: 24,600 lb.
Coal Capacity: 3 tons 10 cwt.
Power Classification: 4–MT.

Additional Identification Features: Most easily identified by Number Series (*q.v.*). Also recognisable from class on page 115 by shorter smoke-box, smaller cylinders, and outside steam-pipes entering smoke-box sides at boiler centre-line. Diamond-shaped slide-bars devoid of large outside motion bracket.

Number Series: 42500 to 42536.

Location: All working on the L.T. & S.R. line between Fenchurch St. and Shoeburyness.

42700–42944

Origin: L.M.S.	*Designers:* George Hughes
Introduced: 1926.	and Sir Henry Fowler.
Driving Wheel: 5 ft. 6 in.	*Purpose:* Mixed Traffic.
Pony Wheel: 3 ft. 6½ in.	*Cylinders (2):* 21 in. × 26 in.
Length: 59 ft. 3⅞ in.	*Boiler Pressure:* 180 lb.sq.in.
Total Weight: 108 tons 4	*Tractive Effort:* 26,580 lb.
cwt.	*Coal Capacity:* 5 tons.
Water Capacity: 3,500 gals.	*Power Classification:* 6-P/5-F.

Additional Identification Features: Of massive appearance with cylinders set very high and at a sharp angle to the footplate, which rises high above them. Note oblong recess in side of cylinder casing. Two glazed windows on each side of cab.

Number Series: 42700 to 42944.

Historical Notes: Designed by Hughes (late of the Lancashire and Yorkshire Railway) and built under the direction of Sir Henry Fowler. Engine Nos. 42818, 42822, 42824, 42825 and 42829 were provided in 1931 with Lentz rotary camshaft valve-gear, but were rebuilt with Reidinger valve-gear in 1953.

Location: Seen on almost all parts of the L.M. Region, more particularly on the lines in the north. About 65 are in Scotland.

• Ex-"5-P/4-F".

STANIER L.M.S. "MOGUL" CLASS   2-6-0

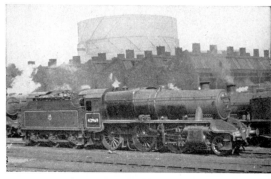

42945–42984

Origin: L.M.S.
Introduced: 1933.
Driving Wheel: 5 ft. 6 in.
Pony Wheel: 3 ft. 3½ in.
Length: 59 ft. 10¾ in.
Total Weight: 111 tons 6 cwt.
Water Capacity: 3,500 gals.
Coal Capacity: 5 tons.

Designer: Sir William Stanier.
Purpose: Mixed Traffic.
Cylinders (2): 18 in. × 26 in.
Boiler Pressure: 225 lb.sq.in.
Tractive Effort: 26,288 lb.
**Power Classification:* 6-P/5-F.

Additional Identification Features: Straight high-level footplate from front of cylinders to front of cab. Two windows to each cab-side. Long back overhang to cab roof. Slanting exhaust pipes from above cylinders to smoke-box. Normal chimney, but "dome" flanked with top-feed pipes and fittings. Tapered boiler. Some engines have safety-valves mounted on the top feed.

Number Series: 42945 to 42984.

Historical Notes: Shows some of the "Swindon" influence brought to the L.M.S. by Sir William Stanier; the coned boiler, for example. Originally these Stanier engines were rated "5-P/4-F", being used on heavy excursion trains in addition to fast heavy freight trains.

Location: All on the former L.N.W.R. lines of the L.M. Region, mostly in the north.

* Old L.M.S. "5-P/4-F" class.

IVATT L.M.S. "MOGUL" (1947) CLASS   2-6-0

43000–43161

Origin: L.M.S.
Introduced: Dec., 1947.
Driving Wheel: 5 ft. 3 in.
Pony Wheel: 3 ft.
Length: 53 ft.
Weight: (Engine) 59 tons 2 cwt.
Designer: H. G. Ivatt.

Purpose: Mixed Traffic.
Cylinders (2): 17½ in. × 26 in.
Boiler Pressure: 225 lb.sq.in.
Tractive Effort: 24,170 lb.
Coal Capacity: 4 tons.
Power Classification: 4–MT.

Additional Identification Features: Very high footplate well clear of cylinders. Cab sides not carried down to tender footplate level. Nos. 43000 to 43049 at first fitted with double chimneys, but all now have single chimneys.

Number Series: 43000 to 43161.

Location: Mostly found on various parts of the M., E. and N.E. Regions.

DEELEY MIDLANDS REBUILDS
(Old "275" Class)

0-6-0

43185–43832

Origin: Midland Railway.
***Introduced:** 1903.
†*Driving Wheel:* 5 ft. 3 in.
Length: 51 ft. 3⅛ in.
Weight: (Engine) 43 tons 3 cwt.
Water Capacity: 3,250 gals.

Designer: Richard M. Deeley.
Purpose: Freight.
Cylinders: 18½ in. × 26 in.
Boiler Pressure: 175 lb. sq. in.
†*Tractive Effort:* 21,010 lb.
Coal Capacity: 4 tons.
Power Classification: 3–F.

Number Series: 43185 to 43832, with gaps in sequence due to scrapping, etc.

Historical Notes: Rebuilds by Deeley and Fowler of Johnson's 1875 design. This once numerous class is now reduced to about 150 engines, and further withdrawals are taking place rapidly. Engines 43194, 43211, 43216, 43218 and 43248 formerly belonged to the Somerset and Dorset Joint Railway.

Location: Found on most parts of the former M.R. system, particularly numerous in the Midlands.

* See Historical Notes.
† Engines 43185/7–9 have 4 ft. 11 in. driving wheels, with 21,240 lb. tractive effort.

MIDLAND FOWLER 4-F CLASS   0-6-0

43835–44026

Origin: Midland Railway.
Introduced: 1911.
Driving Wheel: 5 ft. 3 in.
Designer: Sir Henry Fowler.

Purpose: Freight.
Cylinders: 20 in. × 26 in.
Boiler Pressure: 175 lb.sq.in.
Tractive Effort: 24,555 lb.

Additional Identification Features: At first fitted with earlier Midland type tenders with coal rails, a number of the survivors now have the flat-sided variety.

Number Series: Originally ran from 43835 to 44026, but many have recently been scrapped.

Historical Notes: Class originally introduced by Sir Henry Fowler in 1911, and perpetuated by the L.M.S.R. until 1940, by which time it consisted of no less than 772 engines. Although designed primarily as freight engines, they are often used on passenger trains.

Location: The great majority are stationed on the L.M. Region.

L.M.S. FOWLER 4-F CLASS   0-6-0

44027–44606

Origin: L.M.S.R.
Introduced: 1924.
Driving Wheel: 5 ft. 3 in.
Designer: Sir Henry Fowler.
Purpose: Freight.
Cylinders: 20 in. × 26 in.

Boiler Pressure: 175 lb. sq. in.
Tractive Effort: 24,555 lb.
Power Classification: 4-F.

Number Series: 44027–44606, with gaps due to scrapping.

Historical Notes: Development of M.R. 1911 design as a standard type for the L.M.S.R. Nos. 44557–44561 were built for the Somerset and Dorset Joint Railway as Nos. 57–61, being absorbed into the L.M.S. stock in 1930.

Location: The majority are found on the L.M. Region, but there are a number in all other Regions except the Southern. Nos. 44557–44561 still work over their native S. & D.J.R. section.

"5—MT" CLASS 4-6-0

44658–45499

Origin: L.M.S.
Introduced: Sept., 1934.
Driving Wheel: 6 ft.
Bogie Wheel: 3 ft. 3½ in.
Length: 63 ft. 7¾ in.
Weight: 125 tons 5 cwt.
Water Capacity: 4,000 gals.

Designer: Sir William Stanier.
Purpose: Mixed Traffic.
Cylinders: 18½ in. × 28 in.
Boiler Pressure: 225 lb. sq. in.
Tractive Effort: 25,455 lb.
Coal Capacity: 9 tons.
**Power Classification:* 5—MT.

Additional Identification Features: Straight footplate without driving-wheel splashers. Tapered boiler and flat-topped firebox. Outside cylinders and valve-gear. Curved-in top to tender sides. Some engines have double chimneys and Nos. 44738 to 44757, which are fitted with Caprotti gear, have lower running plates with splashers over the driving wheels (see page 124).

Number Series: 44658 to 45499.

Historical Notes: Very similar to "Jubilee" class but with only two cylinders and smaller diameter driving-wheels. 427 built by outside firms, the first in service being No. 45020, a Vulcan Foundry product: the first from Crewe was No. 45000 in February, 1935. Crewe eventually built 241, Horwich 120, Derby 54, A. W. and Co. 327 and Vulcan Foundry 100. Many engines numbered below 44768 were experimentally modified or designed with various types of valve-gear, roller-bearings, and steel fire-boxes. Among the class, the experimental engines varied in weight from 70 tons 12 cwt. to 75 tons 6 cwt.

Location: Numerous on all parts of the L.M. Region and the former L.M.S. lines in Scotland. Also found to a lesser extent in a few areas on the other Regions.

* 5–P/5–F on S. Region.

"5–MT" CAPROTTI CLASS 4–6–0

44738–44757

Origin: B.R.
Introduced: 1948.
Driving Wheel: 6 ft.
Bogie Wheel: 3 ft. 3½ in.
Length: 63 ft. 7¾ in.
Weight: 125 tons 5 cwt.
Water Capacity: 4,000 gals.

Designer: Sir William Stanier.
Purpose: Mixed Traffic.
Cylinders: 18½ in. × 28 in.
Boiler Pressure: 225 lb.sq.in.
Tractive Effort: 25,455 lb.
Coal Capacity: 9 tons.
Power Classification: 5–MT.

Additional Identification Features: Distinguished from standard class 5–MT by lower running plate and splashers over driving wheels. Also prominent steam pipes between smoke-box and cylinders. Nos. 44755–44757 have double chimneys. Note: engines 44686 and 44687 also have Caprotti valve-gear but are quite unlike the above or the standard engines in appearance, having a very high running plate, indeed, similar to the 43000 class 2–6–0, illustrated on page 119.

Number Series: 44738 to 44757.

Location: Usually to be seen on the main lines between Leeds and Bristol, Leeds and St. Pancras, Manchester and Euston or on the North Wales coast line.

"PATRIOT" CLASS 4–6–0

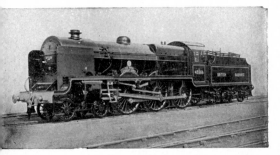

45500–45551

Origin: L.M.S.
Introduced: 1930.
Driving Wheel: 6 ft. 9 in.
Bogie Wheel: 3 ft. 3 in.
Length: 62 ft. 8¾ in.
Weight: 123 tons 9 cwt.
Water Capacity: 3,500 gals.
Designer: Sir Henry Fowler.
Purpose: Express Passenger.

**Cylinders (3):* 18 in. × 26 in.
or 17 in. (see below).
**Boiler Pressure:* 200 lb. sq. in.
or 250 lb. (see below).
**Tractive Effort:* 26,520 lb. or
29,570 lb. (see below).
Coal Capacity: 5¼ tons.
**Power Classification:* 6–P.

Additional Identification Features: Flat-topped Belpaire fire-box and parallel boiler. Rear driving-wheel splashers built into fire-box. Smoke deflector plates at side of smoke-box.

Number Series: 45500 to 45551.

Historical Notes: A 3-cylindered rebuild by Fowler of the old London and North Western "Claughton" class, which was introduced in January, 1913, using the original wheels (Nos. 45500 and 45501). Others (Nos. 45502 to 45551) were new engines built to Fowler's design and introduced in July, 1932. (Officially, Nos. 45502 to 45541 were considered as renewals.) Between October, 1946 and December, 1948, 18 engines (see footnote) were fitted by H. G. Ivatt with double chimneys, new cylinders 17 in. × 26 in., and large tapered boilers, pressed to 250 lb. per sq. in., like the "Taper Scots".

Location: Seen on the main lines of the former L.N.W.R. system of the L.M. Region.

* Nos. 45512, 45514, 45521–2–3, 45525–45532, 45534–5–6, 45540, and 45545 are classed as 7–P, with a tractive effort of 29,570 lb. (See Historical Notes). In their rebuilt form they resemble the "Royal Scot" class in appearance (see page 127).

125

45552–45742

Origin: L.M.S.
Introduced: May, 1934.
Driving Wheel: 6 ft. 9 in.
Bogie Wheel: 3 ft. 3½ in.
Length: 64 ft. 8¾ in.
Weight: 134 tons 4 cwt.
Water Capacity: 4,000 gals.

Designer: Sir William Stanier.
Purpose: Express Passenger.
Cylinders (3): 17 in. × 26 in.
Boiler Pressure: 225 lb. sq. in.
Tractive Effort: 26,610 lb.
Coal Capacity: 9 tons.
Power Classification: 6-P.

Additional Identification Features: Straight raised foot-plate. Splashers over each driving-wheel. Square-topped fire-box. Nameplate over forward driving-wheel splasher. Drop front to footplate. Sloping covers to steam pipes alongside smoke-box.

Number Series: 45552 to 45636 and 45638 to 45742 (TOTAL: 190, of which 29 are Sc. Region stock).

Historical Notes: Appeared in the year of King George V's Jubilee. Improved type of "Patriot" class (*q.v.*) with Stanier-coned boiler and top feed. Nos. 45735–6 rebuilt in 1942 with larger boilers and double chimneys. These later rebuilds are hardly distinguishable from rebuilt "Royal Scots", the cylinders being at a slight angle on the "Jubilees". One standard boiler with double chimney is seen on various engines.

Location: Seen on the main lines of the L.M. and Scottish Regions.

* Nos. 45735–6 were rebuilt in 1942, when their weight was 82 tons (engine). Tractive Effort: 29,570 lb. (Class 7-P). Pressure 250 lb. sq. in. In their rebuilt form they resemble the "Royal Scot" class in appearance (see page 127).

"ROYAL SCOT" CLASS 4-6-0

46100–46170

Origin: L.M.S.
Introduced: July, 1927.
Driving Wheel: 6 ft. 9 in.
Bogie Wheel: 3 ft. 3½ in.
Length: 65 ft. 2¼ in.
Total Weight: 137 tons 13 cwt.*
Water Capacity: 4,000 gals.

Designer: North British Loco. Co.
Purpose: Express Passenger.
Cylinders (3): 18 in. × 26 in.
Boiler Pressure: 250 lb. sq. in.
Tractive Effort: 33,150 lb.
Coal Capacity: 9 tons.
Power Classification: 7-P.

Additional Identification Features: Taper boiler with square-topped fire-box sloping towards front of cab. Double chimney. Straight footplate. Splashers over each driving-wheel with nameplate over forward driver.

Number Series: 46100 to 46170.

Historical Notes: Originally built with parallel boiler. All now rebuilt with Stanier taper boilers. No. 46113 ("Cameronian") made a world's record run by taking a train non-stop from Euston to Glasgow in April, 1928, a distance of 401½ miles. No. 46100 (ex 46152) was sent to Chicago World's Fair in 1933, and afterwards toured 11,194 miles in North America, including crossing the Rocky Mountains unaided with its train.

Location: Seen on the main lines of the L.M. and Scottish Regions.

* Engine only, with taper boiler, 83 tons: No. 46170, renewal of high-pressure engine "Fury" 84 tons 1 cwt.

46200–46212

Origin: L.M.S.
Introduced: June, 1933.
Driving Wheel: 6 ft. 6 in.
Bogie Wheel: 3 ft.
Trailing Wheel: 3 ft. 9 in.
Length: 74 ft. 4¼ in.
Total Weight: 159 tons 3 cwt.
Water Capacity: 4,000 gals.

Designer: Sir William Stanier.
Purpose: Express Passenger.
Cylinders (4): 16¼ in. × 28 in.
Boiler Pressure: 250 lb.sq.in.
Tractive Effort: 40,300 lb.
Coal Capacity: 10 tons.
Power Classification: 8–P.

Additional Identification Features: Square-fronted cab front. Cylinders placed over rear bogie-wheels. Curved nameplate over centre driving-wheel splasher. Normal type of chimney. No open slots in girder under fire-box.

Number Series: 46200 to 46212 omitting 46202.

Historical Notes: Sir William Stanier's first express engine was No. 46200 ("The Princess Royal"), which was the first "Pacific" type to run on the L.M.S., quickly followed by No. 46201. Ten more engines were built in 1935 to this design, but with slight modifications to the motion-work.

Location: These engines work principally on the West Coast main line. Nos. 46201 and 46210 are stationed at Polmadie in the Scottish Region. The others are divided between Camden, Crewe and Liverpool.

"PRINCESS CORONATION" CLASS 4-6-2

46220–46257

Origin: L.M.S.
Introduced: 1938.
Driving Wheel: 6 ft. 9 in.
Bogie Wheel: 3 ft.
Trailing Wheel: 3 ft. 9 in.
Length: 73 ft. 9¼ in.
•*Total Weight:* 161 tons 12 cwt.
Water Capacity: 4,000 gals.

Designer: Sir William Stanier.
Purpose: Express Passenger.
Cylinders (4): 16½ in. × 28 in.
Boiler Pressure: 250 lb. sq. in.
Tractive Effort: 40,285 lb.
Coal Capacity: 10 tons.
Power Classification: 8-P.

Additional Identification Features: Bulbous steam-pipe casing at side of smoke-box behind deflectors. Rectangular name-plate above driving-wheels on boiler-barrel. Nos. 46256 and 46257 have the high running plate carried back to the rear of the cab. All have smoke-deflectors and double chimneys.

Number Series: 46220 to 46257.

Historical Notes: Developed from "Princess Royal" class, having larger tenders. As a result of successful trials between London and Glasgow, a high-speed, streamlined train was put into service and named "Coronation Scot". "Coronation" (No. 46220) achieved 114 m.p.h. in 1937. Nos. 46256 and 46257 were a development by H. G. Ivatt. No. 46229 renumbered and renamed 46220 "Coronation" was in America from January, 1939, until 1946. The names and numbers have again been transposed.

Location: Used principally on the heavy expresses between Euston, Crewe and Glasgow, but occasionally seen as far north as Aberdeen.

• Nos. 46256 and 46257 weigh 23 cwt. more.

IVATT L.M.S. "MOGUL" (1946) CLASS   2-6-0

46400–46527

Origin: L.M.S.	*Designer:* H. G. Ivatt.
Introduced: Dec., 1946.	*Purpose:* Mixed Traffic.
Driving Wheel: 5 ft.	•*Cylinders* (2): 16 in. × 24 in.
Pony Wheel: 3 ft.	*Boiler Pressure:* 200 lb. sq. in.
Length: 53 ft. 1¾ in.	•*Tractive Effort:* 17,400 lb.
Weight: 84 tons 5 cwt.	*Coal Capacity:* 4 tons.
Water Capacity: 3,000 gals.	*Power Classification:* 2–MT.

Additional Identification Features: Nos. 46465–46489 are fitted with narrower and taller chimneys than the rest of the class.

Number Series: 46400 to 46527.

Historical Notes: This class carries the typical Ivatt taper boiler and short L.M.S. type chimney (Nos. 46400 to 46464), whilst the rest of the class have the British Railways tall parallel type, with the exception of Nos. 46465 to 46489, which have tapered chimneys.

Location: Scattered chiefly over the L.M. and N.E. Regions, but Nos. 46460-4 are in Scotland, 46465-9 on the Eastern Region, and 46503-46527 on the Western, principally on the lines of the former Cambrian Railway.

• Nos. 46465 to 46527: Cylinders, 16½ in. × 24 in.; Tractive Effort, 18,510 lb.

"KITSON DOCK SHUNTER" CLASS 0-4-0ST

47000–47009

Origin: L.M.S.
Introduced: Nov., 1932.
Driving Wheel: 3 ft. 10 in.
Length: 26 ft. 4¼ in.
*Weight: 33 tons.
Water Capacity: 800 gals.
Designer: Sir William Stanier and Kitson and Co.

Purpose: Dock Shunting Work.
Cylinders: 15½ in. × 20 in.
Boiler Pressure: 160 lb.sq.in.
Tractive Effort: 14,200 lb.
Coal Capacity: 1 ton.
Power Classification: 0–F.

Additional Identification Features: Saddle-tank over smoke-box and forward portion of boiler, with gap between rear of tank and cab front, where boiler top is visible. Top half of cab set rearward over buffer-beam. Outside cylinders set at an angle to horizontal. Squat chimney and dome with tank filler-cap between them.

Number Series: 47000 to 47009.

Historical Notes: Built by Messrs. Kitson for the L.M.S.R. Nos. 47005 to 47009 were built in 1953. These have larger tanks and coal capacity, and weigh 1 ton more than the first batch.

Location: Two at Bank Hall, two at Staveley, three at Birkenhead, one at Preston, one at Derby. No. 47000 works on the middle section of the Cromford and High Peak line.

* See Historical Notes.

"FOWLER DOCK TANK" CLASS   0–6–0T

47160–47169

Origin: L.M.S.
Introduced: Dec., 1928.
Driving Wheel: 3 ft. 11 in.
Length: 27 ft. 6 in.
Weight: 43 tons 12 cwt.
Water Capacity: 1,000 gals.
Designer: Sir Henry Fowler.

Purpose: Dock Shunting Duties.
Cylinders: 17 in. × 22 in.
Boiler Pressure: 160 lb.sq.in.
Tractive Effort: 18,400 lb.
Coal Capacity: 1 ton 10 cwt.
Power Classification: 2–F.

Additional Identification Features: Short wheel-base. Outside cylinders and valve-gear. Side-tanks have lower front end cut away thus giving access between main-frames.

Number Series: 47160 to 47169. Nos. 47162 and 47169 have been scrapped.

Historical Notes: Of especially short fixed wheel-base (9 ft. 6 in.) for short radius curve work.

Location: To be seen at Fleetwood, Speke Junction and other places on the L.M. Region. Three are in Scotland, two of these being stationed at Greenock.

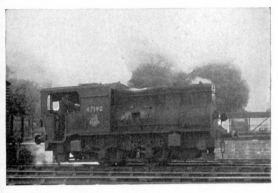

47190

Origin: S. & D.J.R.
Introduced: 1929.
Purpose: Colliery Shunting.
Driving Wheel: 3 ft. 1½ in.

Cylinders (4): 6¾ in × 9 in.
Boiler Pressure: 275 lb.sq.in.
Tractive Effort: 15,500 lb.

Additional Identification Features: Sentinel, 4-wheeled locomotive with chain-driven gears.

Number Series: 47190. A sister engine No. 47191 has now been scrapped.

Historical Notes: Two engines supplied by the Sentinel Wagon Works in 1929 to the Somerset and Dorset Joint Railway, to the requirements of R. C. Archbutt, Locomotive Superintendent.

Location: Radstock.

"JOHNSON LARGE MIDLAND TANK" CLASS
0–6–0T

47200–47259

Origin: Midland Railway.
Introduced: 1899.
Driving Wheel: 4 ft. 7 in.
Length: 31 ft. 4 in.
Weight: 48 tons 15 cwt.
Water Capacity: 1,200 gals.
Designer: S. W. Johnson.

Purpose: Light Freight and Shunting.
Cylinders (2): 18 in. × 26 in.
Boiler Pressure: 160 lb. sq. in.
Coal Capacity: 2 tons 5 cwt.
Power Classification: 3–F.

Additional Identification Features: The forerunner of the standard L.M.S. Fowler shunting tank (see page 135). Some engines have condensing pipes fitted from smoke-box to top of side-tanks.

Number Series: 47200–47259, with gaps due to scrapping.

Historical Notes: All rebuilt with Belpaire fire-boxes from 1919 onwards.

Location: A number in the London area at Cricklewood and Kentish Town, others at various sheds in the L.M. & N.E. Regions.

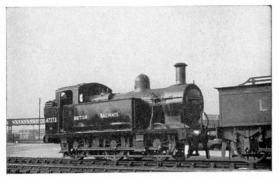

47260–47681

Origin: L.M.S.
Introduced: 1924.
Driving Wheel: 4 ft. 7 in.
Length: 31 ft. 4¾ in.
Weight: 49 tons 10 cwt.
Water Capacity: 1,200 gals.
Designer: Sir Henry Fowler.

Purpose: Shunting and Light Freight.
Cylinders (2): 18 in. × 26 in.
Boiler Pressure: 160 lb. sq. in.
Tractive Effort: 20,830 lb.
Coal Capacity: 2 tons 5 cwt.
Power Classification: 3–F.

Additional Identification Features: Cab fitted with ventilator on roof. Belpaire fire-box. Extended smoke-box.

Number Series: 47260 to 47681, with gaps due to scrapping.

Historical Notes: Engines in this class were developments of earlier Midland Railway designs and were introduced just after grouping. Nos. 47310 to 47316 were built to the same design in 1929 for use on the Somerset and Dorset Joint Railway, but were taken into L.M.S. stock the following year.

Location: Widely scattered throughout the L.M. Region, but also found in a few places on all the other Regions, except the Southern.

"STANIER 8-F" CLASS

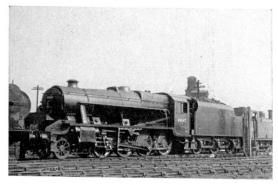

48000–48775

Origin: L.M.S.
Introduced: 1935.
Driving Wheel: 4 ft. 8½ in.
Pony Wheel: 3 ft. 3½ in.
Length: 63 ft. ¾ in.
Total Weight: 125 tons 15 cwt.
Water Capacity: 4,000 gals.
Designer: Sir William Stanier.

Purpose: Heavy Long-distance Freight.
Cylinders (2): 18½ in. × 28 in.
Boiler Pressure: 225 lb. sq. in.
Tractive Effort: 32,440 lb.
Coal Capacity: 9 tons.
Power Classification: 8–F.

Additional Identification Features: Stanier taper boiler with Belpaire fire-box.

Number Series: 48000 to 48775, with gaps due to transfer to War Department for use abroad during the War, and to non-completion of sequences.

Historical Notes: 849 engines were built, many delivered direct to the W.D. without having L.M.S. numbers. N.B.L. Co. built 208, Crewe 136, Brighton 93, Swindon 80, Horwich 75, Vulcan Foundry 67, Darlington 53, Doncaster 50, Beyer Peacock and Co. 50, Eastleigh 23, Ashford 14. Eighty others were completed for the government by N.B.L. Co. as "Austerity" class.

Location: The majority perform heavy freight work over the main lines of the former L.M.S. system.

48895–49454

Origin: L.N.W.R.
Introduced: 1912.
Driving Wheel: 4 ft. 5½ in.
Length: 55 ft. 4 in.
Weight: (Engine) 61 tons (approx.).
Water Capacity: 3,000 gals.

Designer: C. J. Bowen-Cooke.
Purpose: Heavy Freight.
Cylinders: 20½ in. × 24 in.
Boiler Pressure: 175 lb.sq.in.
Tractive Effort: 28,045 lb.
Coal Capacity: 6 tons.
Power Classification: 7–F.

Additional Identification Features: Rectangular bottom cab panel which extends further forward than the cab. Also combined sand-boxes and splashers over the two leading pairs of wheels. Unusual wheels with "H"-section spokes.

Number Series: 48895 to 49454, with gaps due to scrapping.

Historical Notes: A very mixed class of which some engines were originally of old London and North Western "G–1", "G–2" and "G–2a" classes, the latter being introduced as rebuilds of "G–1" class in 1936.

Location: Mostly at work on the former L.N.W.R. lines of the L.M. Region.

"FOWLER 7-F" CLASS 0-8-0

49500–49674

Origin: L.M.S.
Introduced: April, 1929.
Driving Wheel: 4 ft. 8½ in.
Length: 56 ft. 1 in.
Total Weight: 101 tons 19 cwt.
Water Capacity: 3,500 gals.
Designer: Sir Henry Fowler.

Purpose: Heavy Freight.
Cylinders (2): 19½ in. × 26 in.
Boiler Pressure: 200 lb.sq.in.
Tractive Effort: 29,747 lb.
Coal Capacity: 4 tons.
Power Classification: 7-F.

Additional Identification Features: Straight footplate. Belpaire fire-box. Squat chimney and dome. Engine devoid of all visible accessories except for the mechanical lubricator over the front wheels.

Number Series: Originally ran from 49500 to 49674, but only Nos. 49505/8, 49618, 49627, 49637 and 49668 now remain.

Historical Notes: Developed from the old London and North Western "G–2" class, and sometimes referred to as "G–3".

Location: All stationed on the old L. & Y.R. system, and are seen only on local freight work in Lancashire and Yorkshire.

L. & Y. WORKS SHUNTER 0-4-0ST

"WREN"

Origin: L. & Y.R.
Built: 1887.
Gauge: 1 ft. 6 in.
Driving Wheel: 1 ft. 4¼ in.

Weight: 3½ tons.
Cylinders (2): 5 in. × 6 in.
Boiler Pressure: 170 lb.sq.in.

Additional Identification Features: Distinctive engine running on 18-in. gauge system at Horwich works.

Number Series: Unnumbered: named "Wren".

Historical Notes: Small engines built for transporting materials at Horwich works over the 18-in. gauge system. Originally there were eight of them, the others being named "Dot", "Robin", "Fly", "Wasp", "Midget", "Mouse" and "Bee". "Wren" is now the only survivor.

Location: Can only be seen at Horwich works. When not in use there is a small Diesel loco. which deputises.

"L. & Y.R. RADIAL TANK" CLASS   2-4-2T

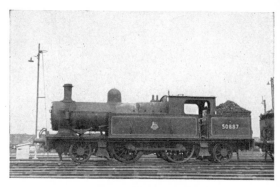

50721, 50746, 50850

Origin: Lancashire and Yorkshire Railway.
Introduced: Feb., 1889.
Driving Wheel: 5 ft. 7⅜ in.
Weight: 55 tons 19 cwt.
Water Capacity: 1,340 gals.
Designers: J. A. Aspinall and G. Hughes.

Purpose: Suburban Passenger.
Cylinders (2): 18 in. × 26 in.
Boiler Pressure: 180 lb.sq.in.
Tractive Effort: 18,954 lb.
Coal Capacity: 2 tons.
Power Classification: 2–P.

Additional Identification Features: Some engines had round-topped fire-boxes, short smoke-boxes and smaller bunkers, whilst others have been rebuilt as illustrated. (This particular engine was built new in this form.)

Number Series: This numerous class ran from 50621 to 50953, but only three survivors now remain.

Historical Notes: Successive introduction in 1892, 1898, 1905 and 1910 resulted in slightly varying weights, cylinder sizes and tractive efforts. This was the old L. & Y. "5" class.

Location: The three remaining engines are stationed in the Southport area.

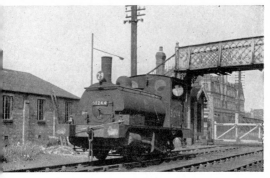

51200–51253

Origin: L. and Y.R.
Introduced: Dec., 1891.
Driving Wheel: 3 ft. ⅞ in.
Weight: 21 tons 5 cwt.
Designer: J. A. F. Aspinall.
Purpose: Dock Shunting
   Duties.

Cylinders: 13 in. × 18 in.
Boiler Pressure: 160 lb. sq.
  in.
Tractive Effort: 11,335 lb.
Power Classification: 0–F.

Additional Identification Features: Disc wheels, covered-in slide-bars, saddle-tank over whole length of boiler, and cab much higher than top of tank. Dumb buffers.

Number Series: 51202–51253, with gaps due to scrapping.

Location: Several are stationed at Bank Hall and may be seen along the waterfront in the Liverpool dock area. Others are to be found at such widely scattered places as Goole and Bristol.

LANCASHIRE AND YORKSHIRE CLASS

0–6–0ST

51336–51524, 11304, 11305, 11324, 11368

Origin: L. and Y.R.
Introduced: 1891.
Driving Wheel: 4 ft. 6 in.
Weight: 43 tons 17 cwt.
Designer: J. A. F. Aspinall.

Purpose: Light Freight and Shunting.
Cylinders (2): $17\frac{1}{2}$ in. × 26 in.
Boiler Pressure: 140 lb.sq.in.
Tractive Effort: 17,545 lb.
Power Classification: 2–F.

Additional Identification Features: Saddle-tank covers boiler but not smoke-box.

Number Series: 51336 to 51524, with gaps due to scrapping. Also four service locomotives at Horwich works (Nos. 11304, 11305, 11324 and 11368).

Historical Notes: Rebuilds of the original Lancashire and Yorkshire " F–15 " class designed by W. Barton-Wright and introduced in August, 1876.

Location: The twenty survivors of this once numerous class are mainly found on shunting duties at various points on the old L. & Y.R. system. Three are in use as works shunters at Crewe, and four others, which for some reason still retain their L.M.S. numbers (as detailed above), are service locomotives at Horwich works.

LANCASHIRE AND YORKSHIRE CLASS

0–6–0T

51537

Origin: L. & Y.R.
Introduced: 1897.
Designer: J. A. F. Aspinall.
Purpose: Colliery and dock shunting.

Driving Wheel: 4 ft.
Cylinders (2): 17 in. × 24 in.
Boiler Pressure: 140 lb.sq.in.
Tractive Effort: 15,285 lb.

Additional Identification Features: Outside cylinders. unusual for a 0–6–0T design.

Number Series: 51537.

Historical Notes: Originally a series of 20 engines built in 1897 for use on lines with sharp curvatures.

Location: At Aintree (Liverpool).

52089–52526

Origin: L. and Y.R.
Introduced: Sept., 1889.
Driving Wheel: 5 ft. 1 in.;
and 4 ft. 7½ in. (Furness).
Length: 48 ft. 9 in.
Water Capacity: 1,800 gals.
Designer: J. A. F. Aspinall.

Purpose: Freight.
Cylinders: 18 in × 26 in.
Tractive Effort: 21,000 lb.
(approx.).
Coal Capacity: 3 tons.
Power Classification: 3-F.

Additional Identification Features: Some engines have been rebuilt with Belpaire fire-boxes, and extended smoke-boxes.

Number Series: 52089 to 52526, with gaps in sequence due to scrapping.

Historical Notes: A once numerous class, of which about 50 still remain.

Location: Mainly found in Lancashire and Yorkshire at former L. & Y.R. sheds, but a few are in North Wales, at Rhyl, and two or three are used as works shunters at Crewe.

53800–53810

Origin: Somerset and Dorset Joint Railway.
Introduced: 1914.
Driving Wheel: 4 ft. 8½ in.
Pony Wheel: 3 ft. 3½ in.
Length: 58 ft. 10⅜ in.
Total Weight: 111 tons 5 cwt.
Water Capacity: 3,500 gals.

Designer: Sir Henry Fowler.
Purpose: Freight.
Cylinders (2): 21 in. × 28 in.
Boiler Pressure: 190 lb. sq. in.
Tractive Effort: 35,296 lb.
Power Classification: 7-F.
Coal Capacity: 5 tons 10 cwt.

Additional Identification Features: Straight footplate, raised (with square corners) over cylinders set at an angle to horizontal. Ventilator on cab roof.

Number Series: 53800 to 53805 built at Derby in 1914; and 53806 to 53810, built by R. Stephenson and Co., with 5 ft. 3 in. diameter boilers, in 1925. No. 53800 has been scrapped.

Historical Notes: Five engines of this class were introduced in 1925. They had a larger boiler than the others which were fitted with 4 ft. 9 in. diameter boilers. All now carry the smaller 4 ft. 9 in. type boiler. On occasions, used for passenger trains.

Location: Confined entirely to the old Somerset and Dorset Joint line between Bath and Bournemouth.

54462–54508

Origin: Caledonian Railway.	*Purpose:* Passenger.
Introduced: 1916.	*Cylinders:* 20½ in. × 26 in.
Driving Wheel: 6 ft. 6 in.	*Boiler Pressure:* 180 lb. sq.
Weight: (Engine) 61 tons	in.
5 cwt.	*Power Classification:* 3–P.
Designer: W. Pickersgill.	*Tractive Effort:* 21,435 lb.

Number Series: 54462–54508, with gaps due to scrapping.

Historical Notes: 54461–6 were built at St. Rollox in 1916, 54467–54476 by N. B. Locomotive Co. in the same year. 54477–54486 built at St. Rollox 1920, 54487–54496 by Armstrong Whitworth and Co. 1921, 54497–54508 by N. B. Loco. Co. 1922.

Location: Some of the engines are on the old Highland system in the far north, the others being found at various points on the former Caledonian Railway.

CALEDONIAN

0-4-4T

55124–55269

Origin: Caledonian Railway.
Introduced: 1895.
Driving Wheel: 5 ft. 9 in.
Trailing Wheel: 3 ft. 2 in.
Length: 33 ft. 11¼ in.
•Weight: 53 tons 19 cwt.
Water Capacity: 1,270 gals.
Designer: J. F. McIntosh.

Purpose: Suburban Passenger.
•Cylinders (2): 18 in. × 26 in.
Boiler Pressure: 180 lb.sq.in.
•Tractive Effort: 18,680 lb.
Coal Capacity: 2 tons 10 cwt.
Power Classification: 2–P.

Additional Identification Features: Most, but not quite all, now carry the stove-pipe chimney as illustrated.

Number Series: 55124, 55126, 55165–55240 with gaps due to scrapping, and 55260–55269.

Historical Notes: A very successful engine which (with detail alterations) was adopted by William Pickersgill from 1915 (see footnote). Nos. 55260–9 built in 1925.

Location: Widely scattered over the Scottish Region.

• Engines introduced by Mr. Pickersgill in 1915 weighed 57 tons 12 cwt. (Nos. 55227 to 55236), and four in 1922 (Nos. 55237 to 55240) weighed 57 tons 17 cwt. having iron front buffer beams for banking at Beattock, etc., and 18½-in. cylinders. Nos. 55237–55240 and 55260–9 (which weigh 59 tons 12 cwt.) have a tractive effort of 19,200 lb.

147

"611" (Caledonian) CLASS

0-4-0ST

56027–56039

Origin: Caledonian Railway.
Introduced: 1895.
Driving Wheel: 3 ft. 8 in.
Length: 22 ft. 3¾ in.
Weight: 27 tons 7½ cwt.
Water Capacity: 800 gals.
Designer: J. F. McIntosh.

Purpose: Dockyard Shunting.
Cylinders (2): 14 in. × 20 in.
Boiler Pressure: 140 lb. sq. in.
**Coal Capacity:* 1 ton 5 cwt.
Tractive Effort: 10,601 lb.
Power Classification: 0–F.

Additional Identification Features: Distinguished from "Y–9" class (page 200) by tall tapering chimney with large flared top.

Number Series: 56027/9, 56031/2/5/9.

Historical Note: Developed from a class originally brought out by Dugald Drummond in 1885.

Location: 56027 and 56032 are works shunters at Crewe. The others are located around Glasgow.

* No normal coal bunker was provided and only a small amount of coal was carried in the cab. When necessary a small four-wheeled wooden wagon was attached as a tender, coal being shovelled by way of a waist-high trap-door in rear-cab sheeting.

"CALEDONIAN DOCK-TANK" CLASS 498
0–6–0T

56151–56173

Origin: Caledonian Railway.
Introduced: 1911.
Driving Wheel: 4 ft.
Length: 26 ft. 9¾ in.
Weight: 47 tons 15 cwt.
Water Capacity: 1,000 gals.
Designer: J. F. McIntosh.

Purpose: Dock Shunting on Sharp Curves.
Cylinders (2): 17 in. × 22 in.
Boiler Pressure: 160 lb.sq.in.
Tractive Effort: 18,014 lb.
Coal Capacity: 2 tons.
Power Classification: 2–F.

Additional Identification Features: Very short fixed wheel-base. Straight footplate. Outside cylinders, mounted horizontally. Some, but not all, have stove-pipe chimneys as illustrated.

Number Series: 56151 to 56173, with gaps due to scrapping.

Historical Notes: These engines had the distinction of being the only type designed by Mr. McIntosh with outside cylinders. They were a great advance on the previous 4-coupled saddle-tanks used in dock areas.

Location: Seen in Scottish dock areas and on local freight services around Glasgow.

CALEDONIAN "29" and "782" CLASSES

0–6–0T

56230–56376

Origin: Caledonian Railway.
Introduced: April, 1895.
Driving Wheel: 4 ft. 6 in.
Length: 30 ft. 10 in.
•*Weight:* 47 tons 15 cwt.
Water Capacity: 1,300 gals.
Designer: J. F. McIntosh.

Purpose: Freight and Shunting.
Cylinders (2): 18 in. × 26 in.
Boiler Pressure: 150 lb.sq.in.
Tractive Effort: 19,890 lb.
Coal Capacity: 2 tons 10 cwt.

Power Classification: 3–F.

Additional Identification Features: Many of the class are now fitted with stove-pipe chimneys.

Number Series: 56230 to 56376, with gaps due to scrapping.

Historical Notes: The old "782" class (Caledonian Railway) was similar to the "29" class in design, but without condensing apparatus. In the "29" class (56231–56236, 56238–9) the pipes can be seen entering the front of the side-tanks from the smoke-box.

Location: Seen on shunting duties on the old Caledonian, G. & S.W.R., and Highland systems.

• With condenser 49 tons 14½ cwt.

CALEDONIAN SMALL GOODS CLASS   0-6-0

57230–57473

Origin: Caledonian Railway.
Introduced: 1883.
Driving Wheel: 5 ft.
Weight: (Engine) 41 tons
6 cwt.
Designer: Dugald Drummond.

Purpose: Main-line Freight.
Cylinders: 18 in. × 26 in.
Boiler Pressure: 180 lb.sq.in.
Tractive Effort: 21,480 lb.
Power Classification: 2–F.

Additional Identification Features: Most of the class now fitted with stove-pipe chimneys, as illustrated.

Number Series: 57230 to 57473, with gaps due to scrapping.

Historical Notes: This was the celebrated Drummond "Standard Goods" class of the Caledonian Railway, upon which engines both J. Lambie and J. F. McIntosh later made additions and modifications.

Location: Seen on local freight work, and sometimes also on passenger trains, throughout the old Caledonian and G. & S.W.R. systems.

"812" (CALEDONIAN CLASS) 0-6-0

57550–57645

Origin: Caledonian Railway.
Introduced: 1899.
Driving Wheel: 5 ft.
Length: 51 ft. 1¾ in.
Weight: 45 tons 14 cwt.
Water Capacity: 3,000 gals.
Designer: J. F. McIntosh.

Purpose: Main-line Freight.
Cylinders (2): 18½ in. × 26 in.
Boiler Pressure: 180 lb.sq.in.
Coal Capacity: 4 tons 10 cwt.
Tractive Effort: 22,690 lb.

Additional Identification Features: Straight footplate. Tapering chimney of medium height. Front splasher merged with square-fronted sand-box, and smoke-box wing-plate.

Number Series: 57550 to 57645, with gaps due to scrapping. Nos. 57550 to 57628 (with gaps) were old Caledonian "812" class, and Nos. 57630 to 57645 (with gaps) were old class "652".

Historical Notes: An enlarged version of the Caledonian Railway "709" class, in which the cab shape follows the design used on the "766" class. This class might well be called the McIntosh "Standard Goods" design.

Location: Mostly on the old Caledonian and G. & S.W.R. systems, with a few on the Highland.

CALEDONIAN RAILWAY "300" CLASS   0-6-0

57650–57691

Origin: Caledonian Railway.
Introduced: Jan., 1918.
Driving Wheel: 5 ft.
Weight: (Engine) 50 tons
  13 cwt.
Designer: William Pickersgill.

Purpose: Freight.
Cylinders: 18½ in. × 26 in.
Boiler Pressure: 180 lb.sq.in.
Tractive Effort: 22,690 lb.
Power Classification: 3–F.

Number Series: 57650–57691, with gaps due to scrapping.

Historical Notes: An enlarged development of the previous McIntosh design.

Location: All on the former Caledonian and G. & S.W.R. systems.

58086

Origin: Midland Railway.
Introduced: 1881.
Driving Wheel: 5 ft. 4 in.
Weight: 53 tons 4 cwt.
Designer: S. W. Johnson.
Purpose: Light Passenger.

Cylinders: 18 in. × 24 in.
Boiler Pressure: 140/150 lb. sq. in.
Tractive Effort: 15,000 lb (approx.).
Power Classification: 1–P.

Number Series: 58086.

Historical Notes: Johnson's standard suburban passenger tank engine, the class originally consisting of 205 engines.

Location: The last survivor of this class is allocated to the Somerset and Dorset section.

58114–58310

Origin: Midland Railway.
Introduced: 1875; with Belpaire firebox, 1917.
Driving Wheel: 5 ft. 3 in.
Weight: (Engine) 39 tons (approx.).
Water Capacity: 2,950 gals.

Designer: S. W. Johnson.
Purpose: Freight.
Cylinders: 18 in. × 26 in.
Boiler Pressure: 160 lb.sq.in.
Tractive Effort: 18,185 lb.
Coal Capacity: 4 tons.
Power Classification: 2–F.

Additional Identification Features: Many still have the earlier Johnson type of cab, but the tender cab carried by the engine illustrated is unusual.

Number Series: 58114 to 58310, with gaps in sequence due to scrapping.

Historical Notes: A once exceedingly numerous class, consisting of nearly 1,000 engines. Many were rebuilt to class "3" (see page 120), and about 50 of the un-rebuilt engines still remain. Although not quite the oldest engines still at work on B.R. (see pages 74 and 99), they are the oldest class still remaining in any considerable numbers, as no less than 28 of the original 120 engines built in 1875 and 1876 are in service.

Location: Widely scattered over the former Midland system. A number may also be found at Barrow, and several others are used for shunting in L.N.W.R. yards in the Birmingham area.

58850

Origin: North London Railway.

Introduced: 1887.

Driving Wheel: 4 ft. 4 in.

Weight: 45 tons 10 cwt.

Designer: J. C. Park.

Purpose: Light Suburban Freight.

Cylinders (2): 17 in. × 24 in.

Boiler Pressure: 160 lb.sq.in.

Tractive Effort: 18,140 lb.

Power Classification: 2–F.

Additional Identification Features: Inside bunker at rear of cab. Outside cylinders. Square "splashers" over front pair of driving-wheels. No outside valve-gear.

Number Series: 58850.

Historical Notes: The 30 engines of this class, together with the 4–4–0 passenger engines of the North London Railway "67" class, at one time formed the two standard classes of locomotive on that railway. No. 58850 is now the last surviving engine from that railway.

Location: Until recently, engines of this class were used on the Cromford and High Peak lines, but they have now been displaced by class "J94". No. 58850 still remains at Rowsley, however, at the time of going to press.

60001–60034

Origin: L.N.E.R.
Introduced: Sept., 1935.
Driving Wheel: 6 ft. 8 in.
Bogie Wheel: 3 ft. 2 in.
Trailing Wheel: 3 ft. 8 in.
Length: 71 ft. ⅜ in.
Total Weight: 165 tons 7 cwt.
Tender Weight: 64 tons 19 cwt., but corridor tender weight 60 tons 7 cwt.
Water Capacity: 5,000 gals.
Designer: Sir Nigel Gresley.

Purpose: Express Passenger
Cylinders (3): 18½ in. × 26 in. Inside cylinder 17 in. in a few cases.
Boiler Pressure: 250 lb.sq.in.
Tractive Effort: 35,455 lb. (or 33,616 lb., with 17 in. inside cylinder).
Coal Capacity: 8 tons.
Power Classification: 8–P / 6–F.
Route Availability: 9.

Additional Identification Features: Streamlined casing. Vee-fronted cab, and cylinders placed between bogie wheels.

Number Series: 60001 to 60034.

Historical Notes: Regarded as Sir Nigel Gresley's masterpiece, the "A–4's" are based on the design of the famous "Great Northern" 4–6–2, as high-speed engines for specially fast running between London and Newcastle. One of these "A–4's", "Mallard", achieved a world record for steam locomotives of 126 m.p.h. on July 3, 1938. 126 m.p.h. was maintained for 5 miles with a seven-coach train.

Location: On East Coast main line between King's Cross and Edinburgh.

A-3 "PACIFIC" 4-6-2

60035–60112

Origin: G.N.R.
Introduced: 1922.
Driving Wheel: 6 ft. 8 in.
Bogie Wheel: 3 ft. 2 in.
Trailing Wheel: 3 ft. 8 in.
Length: 70 ft. 5 in.
Total Weight: 154 tons 3 cwt.
Water Capacity: 5,000 gals.

Designer: Sir Nigel Gresley.
Purpose: Express Passenger.
Cylinders (3): 19 in × 26 in.
Boiler Pressure: 220 lb. sq. in.
Tractive Effort: 32,910 lb.
Coal Capacity: 8 tons.
Power Classification: 7-P/6-F.
Route Availability: 9.

Additional Identification Features: Distinguishable from the present "A-1" class by the absence of the smoke deflectors (except on No. 60097) present on class "A-1".

Number Series: 60035 to 60112. No. 60104 has recently been scrapped.

Historical Notes: A development of Gresley's 1922 "Pacific" (originally classed as "A-1") these engines were designed to haul the fastest and heaviest trains on the L.N.E.R. They were virtually "A-1's" fitted with new boilers working at 220 lb. instead of 180 lb., as was the case with their predecessors.

Location: To be seen anywhere on the East Coast main lines between King's Cross and Aberdeen.

60113–60162

Origin: L.N.E.R.
Introduced: 1945 and 1948.
Driving Wheel: 6 ft. 8 in.
Bogie Wheel: 3 ft. 2 in.
Trailing Wheel: 3 ft. 8 in.
Length: 72 ft. 10⅝ in.
Total Weight: 164 tons 9 cwt.
Water Capacity: 5,000 gals.

Designers: Edward Thompson, A. H. Peppercorn.
Purpose: Express Passenger.
Cylinders (3): 19 in × 26 in.
Boiler Pressure: 250 lb. sq. in.
Tractive Effort: 37,400 lb.
Coal Capacity: 9 tons.
Power Classification: 8–P/6–F.
Route Availability: 9.

Additional Identification Features: Non-streamlined, but fitted with smoke-screens carrying nameplates and double chimneys. Distinguishable from "A-3's" by almost vertical ends to front ends of main-frame over front buffer-beam. Footplate angled to clear driving wheels, over which hardly any splashers are visible. Distinction from class A-2 (page 160): outside cylinders *between* bogie and coupled wheels.

Number Series: 60113 to 60162.

Historical Notes: One engine in this class (No. 60113) was a rebuild of the original "A-1" class (later reclassed as "A-10") by Thompson, Sir Nigel Gresley's successor. The rest were developments of the Thompson rebuild. Nos. 60153 to 60157, were fitted with roller-bearings.

Location: To be seen anywhere on the East Coast main lines between King's Cross and Aberdeen.

* 161 tons 7 cwt. in the case of No. 60113 (A-1/1).

A–2/3 "PACIFIC"

60500–60539

Origin: L.N.E.R.
Introduced: 1943.
Driving Wheel: 6 ft. 2 in.
Bogie Wheel: 3 ft. 2 in.
Trailing Wheel: 3 ft. 8 in.
Length: 71 ft. 7⅜ in.
*Total Weight: 161 tons 17 cwt.
Water Capacity: 5,000 gals.
Designer: Edward Thompson.

Purpose: Express Passenger.
†Cylinders (3): 20 in × 26 in.
† Boiler Pressure: 225 lb. sq. in.
†Tractive Effort: 40,320 lb.
Coal Capacity: 9 tons.
Power Classification: 8–P/6–F
(excepting Nos. 60507 to
60510 which are 7–P/6–F).
Route Availability: 9.

Additional Identification Features: Footplating stepped up in a curve alongside smoke-box, cylinders set between rear bogie-wheel and leading driving-wheel. Nos. 60500 to 60524 have double chimneys and blast-pipes. No splashers over driving-wheels.

Number Series: 60500 to 60539.

Historical Notes: Some (Nos. 60501 to 60506) are rebuilds from Gresley class P–2 (2–8–2), others being then built to a similar design with a V–2 (2–6–2) boiler (Nos. 60507 to 60510). An entirely new version produced by Thompson had a boiler pressure of 250 lb. sq. in. (Nos. 60511 to 60524). A. H. Peppercorn improved still further upon the class producing Nos. 60525–60539 with a slightly shorter wheel-base. Some of these latter engines were again rebuilt with a double blast-pipe (60526/9, 60532/3/8/9).

Location: To be seen anywhere on the East Coast main lines between King's Cross and Aberdeen.

* Tender weight 60 tons 7 cwt. (except Nos. 60509–10: 52 tons).
† Class A–2/2 Nos. 60501 to 60506). A–2/1 have 19-in. cyls. and tractive effort 36,385 lb. A–2/3 have 19-in. cyls. and 250 lb. pressure. TE 40,430 lb. introduced May, 1946.

"V-2" CLASS

2-6-2

60800–60983

Origin: L.N.E.R.
Introduced: June, 1936.
Driving Wheel: 6 ft. 2 in.
Pony Wheel: 3 ft. 2 in.
Trailing Wheel: 3 ft. 8 in.
Length: 66 ft. 5¼ in.
***Weight:* 93 tons 2 cwt.
Water Capacity: 4,200 gals.

Designer: Sir Nigel Gresley.
Purpose: Fast Mixed Traffic.
Cylinders (3): 18½ in. × 26 in.
Boiler Pressure: 220 lb. sq. in.
Tractive Effort: 33,730 lb.
Coal Capacity: 7 tons 10 **cwt.**
Power Classification: 7–P/6–F.
Route Availability: 9.

Additional Identification Features: Nameplates, where fitted,
over centre pair of driving-wheels, excepting on No. 60800, which
has rectangular plates on the smoke-box sides. Footplate raised
over cylinders, then upswept over driving-wheels, returning to
normal level under fire-box and cab. No outside steam-pipes.

Number Series: 60800 to 60983.

Historical Notes: A numerous class of which "Green Arrow"
(No. 60800) was the first engine to be introduced. Only a few of
this class carry names. Generally used as MT locomotives and
originally designed to handle fast freight traffic.

Location: To be seen anywhere on the East Coast main lines
between King's Cross and Aberdeen.

* Tender extra, 52 tons.

12—R.L

161

"B-1" CLASS 4-6-0

61000–61409

Origin: L.N.E.R.
Introduced: 1942.
Driving Wheel: 6 ft. 2 in.
Bogie Wheel: 3 ft. 2 in.
Length: 61 ft. 7⅞ in.
Total Weight: 123 tons 3 cwt.
Water Capacity: 4,200 gals.
Designer: Edward Thompson.

Purpose: Standard General Utility.
Cylinders (2): 20 in. × 26 in.
Boiler Pressure: 225 lb. sq. in.
Tractive Effort: 26,878 lb.
Coal Capacity: 7½ tons.
Power Classification: 5–MT.
Route Availability: 5.

Additional Identification Features: Straight footplate from cab front to cylinders. No splashers over driving-wheels. Nameplate (if named) on smoke-box immediately over steam-pipes.

Number Series: 61000 to 61409 of which 40 are named after species of antelope and 18 after L.N.E.R. directors. No. 61057 was withdrawn in 1950 after being involved in an accident.

Historical Notes: Known as the "Antelope" class and designed to reduce the number of types of 4–6–0 locomotives. Suitable for all but the very heaviest trains. First 40 built at Darlington, and most of the remainder by the North British Locomotive Company at Glasgow, though 50 came from the Vulcan Foundry and others from the Company's shops at Gorton and Darlington.

Location: Found all over the Eastern, North Eastern and former L.N.E.R. parts of the Scottish Region.

61410–61478

Origin: N.E.R.
Introduced: 1919.
Driving Wheel: 5 ft. 8 in.
Bogie Wheel: 3 ft. 1¼ in.
Length: 62 ft. 6 in.
Total Weight: 124 tons (approx.).
Water Capacity: 4,125 gals.
Designer: Sir Vincent Raven.

Purpose: Mixed Traffic.
Cylinders (3): 18½ in. × 26 in.
Boiler Pressure: 180 lb.sq.in.
Tractive Effort: 30,031 lb.
Coal Capacity: 5¼ tons.
Power Classification: 5–MT.
Route Availability: 7.

Additional Identification Features: Deep cab, similar to L.N.E.R. Standard type. Outside cylinders without outside valve-gear. Splashers to all driving-wheels. Glazed windows to cab sides.

Number Series: 61410 to 61478 (except for rebuilt engines. See next page) and with gaps due to scrapping.

Historical Notes: Originally introduced for handling heavy passenger traffic on the North Eastern Railway. Some rebuilt to "B-16/2" by Gresley, 1937 to 1940, and others (with 3 Walschaerts gears) to "B-16/3" by Thompson, 1944 to 1947 (see opposite).

Location: All stationed in the North Eastern Region, but sometimes to be seen in other Regions.

61417–61476

Origin: N.E.R.
Introduced: 1937 (Gresley). 1944 (Thompson).
Driving Wheel: 5 ft. 8 in.
Bogie Wheel: 3 ft. 1¼ in.
Length: 62 ft. 6 in.
Total Weight: 124 tons (approx.).
Water Capacity: 4,125 gals.

Purpose: Mixed Traffic.
Cylinders (3): 18½ in. × 26 in.
Boiler Pressure: 180 lb.sq.in.
Tractive Effort: 30,031 lb.
Coal Capacity: 5¼ tons.
Power Classification: 5–MT.
Route Availability: 7.

Additional Identification Features: Distinguished from the un-rebuilt engines by higher running plate, outside Walschaerts valve-gear and absence of splashers.

Number Series: 61421, 61435, 61438, 61455, 61457 and 61475 (Gresley rebuilds with Walschaerts valve-gear with derived motion for inside cylinder). 61417, 61418, 61420, 61434, 61439, 61444, 61448, 61449, 61453, 61454, 61461, 61463, 61464, 61467, 61468, 61472 and 61476 (Thompson rebuilds with individual Walschaerts gear for each cylinder).

Location: All stationed in the North Eastern Region, but are sometimes to be seen in other regions.

"B-12/3" CLASS   4-6-0

61572

Origin: G.E.R.
*Introduced: 1911 (1932).
Driving Wheel: 6 ft. 6 in.
Bogie Wheel: 3 ft. 3 in.
Length: 57 ft. 9 in.
Total Weight: 108 tons 16 cwt.
Water Capacity: 3,670 gals.
Designer: S. D. Holden.

Purpose: Express Passenger.
Cylinders (2): 20 in. × 28 in.
Boiler Pressure: 180 lb.sq.in.
Tractive Effort: 21,969 lb.
Coal Capacity: 4 tons.
Power Classification: 4–P/3–F.
Route Availability: 4.

Additional Identification Features: Rear driving-wheels under cab. Inside cylinders. Upswept footplating over coupled wheels. Cab extended well to the rear.

Number Series: Originally ran from 61500 to 61580.

Historical Notes: The original Holden "B-12's" were built to handle the heavily-loaded continental trains from Liverpool Street to Harwich (Parkeston Quay), and did well on that very difficult road.

Location: The last survivor of this class is stationed at Norwich.

* The survivors were rebuilt by Gresley from May, 1932.

61668

Origin: L.N.E.R.
Introduced: Dec., 1928.
Driving Wheel: 6 ft. 8 in.
Bogie Wheel: 3 ft. 2 in.
Length: 62 ft. 2 in.
Total Weight: 129 tons 15 cwt.
Water Capacity: 4,200 gals.
Designer: Sir Nigel Gresley.
Purpose: Express Passenger.

Cylinders (3): 17½ in. × 26 in.
Boiler Pressure: 225 lb. sq. in.
Tractive Effort: 28,555 lb.
Coal Capacity: 7½ tons.
Power Classification: 4-MT (Nos. 61669 and 61670 5P/4F).
Route Availability: 5.

Additional Identification Features: Footplate upswept over driving-wheels. Splashers over driving-wheels. Curved nameplate over centre splasher. Larger driving-wheels than "B-1".

Number Series: The class ran from 61600 to 61672.

Historical Notes: Of typical Gresley design, the "B-17's" or "Sandringhams" were to replace the "B-12's" on the Eastern Section, on which they were very successful between Liverpool Street and Norwich—114 miles in 135 minutes. Nos. 61659 and 61670 were at one time streamlined, but the casing was removed in 1951.

Location: The last survivor of this class is allocated to Stratford.

"K-2" CLASS

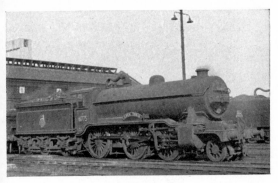

61720–61794

Origin: G.N.R.
Introduced: April, 1914.
Driving Wheel: 5 ft. 8 in.
Pony Wheel: 3 ft. 2 in.
Length: 57 ft. 1½ in.
Total Weight: 107 tons 10 cwt.
Water Capacity: 3,500 gals.
Designer: Sir Nigel Gresley.

Purpose: Mixed Traffic.
Cylinders (2): 20 in. × 26 in.
Boiler Pressure: 180 lb. sq. in.
Tractive Effort: 23,400 lb.
Coal Capacity: 6 tons 10 cwt.
Power Classification: 4–MT.
Route Availability: 5.

Number Series: 61720 to 61794, with gaps due to scrapping.

Additional Identification Features: Nos. 61764, 61772, 61774–5, 61781–2–3, 61787 to 61791 and 61794 are fitted with cab side-windows and are named after Scottish lochs. 61733–4–5, 61741, 61755–8, 61769, 61770–6–9, 61784–5–6, 61792–3 are similarly fitted, but are not named.

Location: All the engines with side window cabs are in Scotland, mostly at Glasgow. The remainder of the class is on the Eastern Region, largely in the Lincolnshire area.

"K-3" CLASS

61800–61992

Origin: G.N.R.
Introduced: March, 1920.
Driving Wheel: 5 ft. 8 in.
Pony Wheel: 3 ft. 2 in.
Length: 59 ft. 6 in.
Total Weight: 124 tons 12 cwt.
Water Capacity: 4,200 gals.
Designer: Sir Nigel Gresley.

Purpose: Medium Freight.
Cylinders (3): 18½ in. × 26 in.
Boiler Pressure: 180 lb. sq. in.
Tractive Effort: 30,030 lb.
Coal Capacity: 7 tons 12 cwt.
Power Classification: 6—MT.
Route Availability: 8.

Additional Identification Features: Massive boiler 6 ft. in diameter with squat chimney and dome. Footplate curved upwards from front buffer-beam and thence again raised above driving-wheels. No splashers. Short exhaust steam pipes at side of smoke-box. Round-topped fire-box. The first ten, built at Doncaster, had the G.N. pattern cab (3,500-gal. tenders when new).

Number Series: 61800 to 61992, with gaps due to scrapping.

Location: On the East Coast main lines and many secondary lines between King's Cross and Aberdeen, and on other parts of the former L.N.E.R. system.

"K-4" CLASS

61993–61998

Origin: L.N.E.R. (for West Highland Line).
Introduced: Jan., 1937.
Driving Wheel: 5 ft. 2 in.
Pony Wheel: 3 ft. 2 in.
Total Weight: 112 tons 12 cwt.
Water Capacity: 3,500 gals.
Designer: Sir Nigel Gresley.

Purpose: Mixed Traffic.
Cylinders (3): 18½ in. × 26 in.
Boiler Pressure: 200 lb.sq.in.
Tractive Effort: 36,600 lb.
Coal Capacity: 6 tons.
Power Classification: 6–P/ 6–F.
Route Availability: 6.

Additional Identification Features: Footplate swept upwards from buffer-beam to front of smoke-box, with slight further curvature over the three coupled axles, then gently downwards to original level to match tender. No splashers. Nameplates on sides of smoke-box. Outside straight steam-pipes between cylinders and smoke-box.

Number Series: 61993 to 61998, excepting 61997 which became the prototype "K-1" class in November, 1945 (see p. 170).

Historical Notes: Designed by Sir Nigel Gresley for working on the West Highland line.

Location: All now stationed at Thornton Junction.

"K-1" CLASS*   2-6-0

61997, 62001–62070

Origin: L.N.E.R.
Introduced: 1949.
Driving Wheel: 5 ft. 2 in.
Pony Wheel: 3 ft. 2 in.
†*Total Weight:* 111 tons 1 cwt.
Water Capacity: 3,500 gals.
Designer: A. H. Peppercorn.
Purpose: Mixed Traffic.

Cylinders (2): 20 in. × 26 in.
Boiler Pressure: 225 lb. sq. in.
Tractive Effort: 32,080 lb.
Coal Capacity: 6 tons.
Power Classification: 6–MT (6–P/6–F).
Route Availability: 6.

Additional Identification Features: Straight footplate above driving-wheels (devoid of splashers) but swept downwards at that point to lower level below cab-side. Break in footplate between raised portion over the driving-wheels and lower part ahead of the cylinders, excepting No. 61997, which has an upswept footplate at this point. No. 61997 carries a nameplate.

Number Series: 61997 and 62001 to 62070.

Historical Notes: The main "K-1" class were developed from No. 61997 (which was rebuilt by Thompson in 1945 as a development of the "K-4" class) for new construction, the length of the engines being increased, and two cylinders taking the place of the previous three used by Sir Nigel Gresley.

Location: Nos. 61997, 62011/2, 62031/4 and 62052 are in Scotland and work over the West Highland line. The others are in the Eastern and North Eastern Regions, a considerable number being stationed at March.

*Illustration is of Class K-1/1, of which No. 61997 is the sole representative.
† No. 61997 somewhat lighter than the standard class.

62467–62496

Origin: North British Railway.
Introduced: 1913.
Driving Wheel: 6 ft.
Bogie Wheel: 3 ft. 6 in.
Length: 56 ft. 3 in.
Total Weight: 103 tons 17 cwt.
Water Capacity: 4,235 gals.

Designer: W. P. Reid.
Purpose: Passenger.
Cylinders (2): 20 in. × 26 in.
Boiler Pressure: 165 lb.sq.in.
Tractive Effort: 20,260 lb.
Coal Capacity: 7 tons.
Power Classification: 3–P.
Route Availability: 6.

Number Series: 62467, 62474/9, 62484/8, 62495/6.

Historical Notes: The celebrated North British Railway "Glen" class, named after Scottish glens, originally consisting of 32 engines. No. 62469 has been restored to its N.B.R. style as No. 256 (see page 31).

Location: The few survivors of this class are scattered over various sheds of the former N.B.R. and G.N.O.S.R. systems.

62613

Origin: G.E.R.	*Purpose:* Passenger.
Introduced: 1933.	*Cylinders* (2): 19 in. × 26 in.
Driving Wheel: 7 ft.	*Boiler Pressure:* 180 lb.sq.in.
Bogie Wheel: 3 ft. 9 in.	*Tractive Effort:* 17,096 lb.
Length: 53 ft. 2 in.	*Coal Capacity:* 5 tons.
Total Weight: 95 tons 3 cwt.	*Power Classification:* 2–P/
Water Capacity: 3,450 gals.	1–F.
Designer: James Holden, re-	*Route Availability:* 5.
built Gresley.	

Additional Identification Features: The last survivor of this class still retains the decorative coupling rod splasher. Many of the later rebuilds had lost this distinctive feature of the original design.

Number Series: The class originally ran from 62500 to 62620.

Historical Notes: The first engine was the famous "Claud Hamilton" exhibited at Paris in 1900.

Location: Stationed at March.

"D–11/2" CLASS 4-4-0

62660–62694

Origin: G.C.R.
Introduced: Dec., 1919.
Driving Wheel: 6 ft. 9 in.
Bogie Wheel: 3 ft. 6 in.
Length: 58 ft. 11½ in.
Total Weight: 109 tons 9 cwt.
Water Capacity: 4,000 gals.
Designer: J. G. Robinson.

Purpose: Passenger.
Cylinders (2): 20 in. × 26 in.
Boiler Pressure: 180 lb.sq.in.
Tractive Effort: 19,644 lb.
Coal Capacity: 6 tons.
Power Classification: 3–P/
2–F.
Route Availability: 6.

Additional Identification Features: Oval buffers. Single splasher over both driving-wheels, with name thereon. Glazed cab side-windows. Nos. 62660–62670, Class "D–11/1", have horizontal nameplates at the edge of the splashers—the remainder, which are Class "D–11/2", have the name painted horizontally as in the illustration.

Number Series: 62660 to 62694, with gaps due to scrapping.

Historical Notes: Introduced originally as the "Large Director" class, which was a development of the 1913 "Director" class. Further engines were constructed in 1924, in L.N.E.R. days, specially modified for Scottish loading gauge and named after characters in Sir Walter Scott's novels.

Location: Nos. 62660–62670 are all in the Sheffield area. Nos. 62671–62694 have always been in the Scottish Region, but most of the survivors are in store and unlikely to run again.

62700–62775

Origin: L.N.E.R.
Introduced: 1927.
Driving Wheel: 6 ft. 8 in.
Bogie Wheel: 3 ft. 1¼ in.
Length: 58 ft. 8¾ in.
Weight: 64 tons (approx.).
Water Capacity: 4,200 gals.
Designer: Sir Nigel Gresley.

Purpose: Light Express Passenger.
Cylinders (3): 17 in. × 26 in.
Boiler Pressure: 180 lb.sq.in.
Tractive Effort: 21,555 lb.
Coal Capacity: 7 tons 10 cwt.
Power Classification: 4–P.
Route Availability: 8.

Additional Identification Features: "Shire" class ("D–49/1") have Walschaerts outside valve-gear, and "Hunt" class ("D–49/2") rotary camshaft gear.

Number Series: 62700 to 62775, with gaps due to scrapping.

Historical Notes: The first 36 engines carried the names of shires through which the L.N.E.R. ran, whilst the remainder (built 1932–1935) bore the names of famous fox-hunting packs. These were generally known as "Shires" and "Hunts" respectively. All were built at Darlington. Two of the first 36 engines had rotary gear (Nos. 62726–7) and in 1932 were renamed after "Hunts"

Location: Divided between the North Eastern and Scottish Regions. Never seen south of Doncaster.

"Q-6" CLASS   0-8-0

63340–63459

Origin: North Eastern Railway.
Introduced: 1913.
Driving Wheel: 4 ft. 7½ in.
Length: 59 ft. 5¼ in.
Total Weight: 110 tons.
Water Capacity: 4,125 gals.
Designer: Sir Vincent Raven.

Purpose: Heavy Main-line Freight.
Cylinders (2): 20 in. × 26 in.
Boiler Pressure: 180 lb.sq.in.
Tractive Effort: 28,800 lb.
Coal Capacity: 5 tons 10 cwt.
Power Classification: 6–F.
Route Availability: 6.

Additional Identification Features: Distinctions from "Q–7" class engines are taller chimney and front sandboxes flanking smoke-box saddle. Outside cylinders drive on third pair of wheels from front end. ("Q–7's" drive on second pair.) Cylinders not set at such a sharp angle to horizontal as on "Q–7" class.

Number Series: 63340 to 63459.

Historical Notes: Built at Darlington, except the last fifty, by Armstrong Whitworth and Co. in 1919/20.

Location: Confined entirely to the North Eastern Region.

63460–63474

Origin: North Eastern Railway.

Introduced: 1919.

Driving Wheel: 4 ft. 7¼ in.

Length: 61 ft. 3 in.

Total Weight: 115 tons 14 cwt.

Water Capacity: 4,125 gals.

Designer: Sir Vincent Raven.

Purpose: Heavy Main-line Freight.

Cylinders (3): 18½ in. × 26 in.

Boiler Pressure: 180 lb.sq.in.

Tractive Effort: 36,965 lb.

Coal Capacity: 5 tons 10 cwt.

Power Classification: 8–F.

Route Availability: 7.

Additional Identification Features: Footplate upswept over outside cylinders, thence straight to front of cab and down again to rear buffer-beam. Cylinders set at angle to horizontal. Boiler devoid of all fittings other than small chimney, a dome and safety-valves. No wheel splashers. Two openings on each cab-side, one of which is glazed.

Number Series: 63460 to 63474.

Location: Confined entirely to the North Eastern Region.

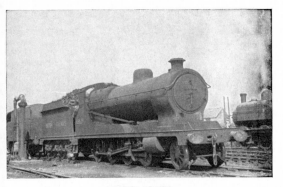

63570–63920

Origin: G.C.R.
Introduced: 1911.
Driving Wheel: 4 ft. 8 in.
Weight: From 72 tons 10 cwt.
to 74 tons 13 cwt.
Designer: J. G. Robinson.

Purpose: Heavy Main-line Freight.
Cylinders (2): 21 in. × 26 in.
Boiler Pressure: 180 lb. sq. in.
Tractive Effort: 31,325 lb.
Power Classification: 7-F.
Route Availability: 6.

Additional Identification Features: There are several varieties of this class, the differences mainly being the type of boiler carried, some of which have round-topped fire-boxes.

Number Series: Nos. 63570 to 63920, with gaps due to conversion to class "O-1" (see page 178), and more recently with other blanks due to scrapping.

Historical Notes: Many engines of this class were built during the first world war for the Government and were later disposed of.

Location: All on the Eastern Region, mostly in the Midlands.

"O–1" CLASS

63571–63901

Origin: Rebuild of G.C.R. "O–4" class (see p. 177).
Introduced: March, 1944.
Driving Wheel: 4 ft. 8 in.
Weight:
  (Engine) 73 tons 6 cwt.
  (Tender) 47 tons 6 cwt., plus 1 ton with scoop.
Water Capacity: 4,000 gals.

Designer of rebuild: E. Thompson.
Purpose: Heavy Main-line Freight.
Cylinders (2): 20 in. × 26 in.
Boiler Pressure: 225 lb.sq.in.
Tractive Effort: 35,520 lb.
Power Classification: 8–F.
Route Availability: 6.

Additional Identification Features: Footplate raised from front of cylinders to front of cab, doing away with need for splashers.

Number Series: 63571/8/9, 63589–92/4/6, 63610/9, 63630, 63644–7, 63650/2, 63663, 63670/6/8, 63687/9, 63711/2, 63725, 63740/6, 63752/5, 63760/8, 63773/7, 63780/4/6/9, 63792/5/6, 63803/6/8, 63817, 63838, 63854/6, 63863/5/7–9, 63872/4/9, 63886/7, 63890, 63901.

Historical Notes: Rebuilt from class "O–4" (see page 177).

Location: All are on the Eastern and North Eastern Regions, mostly in the Midlands around Nottingham, Sheffield, etc.

63922–63987

Origin: G.N.R.
Introduced: 1921.
Driving Wheel: 4 ft. 8 in.
Pony Wheel: 2 ft. 8 in.
Length: 53 ft. 3 in.
●Weight: 74 tons 2 cwt. to 78 tons 13 cwt.
Water Capacity: 4,200 gals.
Designer: Sir Nigel Gresley.

Purpose: Heavy Main-line Freight.
Cylinders (3): 18½ in. × 26 in.
Boiler Pressure: 180 lb. sq. in.
Tractive Effort: 36,470 lb.
Coal Capacity: 7 tons 10 cwt.
Power Classification: 8–F.
Route Availability: 6.

Additional Identification Features: There are four minor varieties to this class, in each of which minor details were altered or added to the original design. Footplate raised over driving-wheels. Normal short chimney and dome. Round-topped fire-box. Some engines with cab side-windows and some without.

Number Series: 63922 to 63987.

Historical Notes: The Gresley 3-cylinder type, further altered in 1924, 1932 and 1943. This class of engine made it possible to run 80-wagon coal trains between London and Peterborough.

Location: All on the Eastern Region, the majority of them at Doncaster.

● Tender extra: Nos. 63922 to 63946, 43 tons 2 cwt.; Nos. 63947 to 63987, 52 tons.

"J–6" CLASS 0–6–0

64170–64279

Origin: G.N.R.
Introduced: 1911.
Driving Wheel: 5 ft. 2 in.
Total Weight: 93 tons 12 cwt.
Water Capacity: 3,000 gals.
Designers: H. A. Ivatt and Sir Nigel Gresley.
• *Purpose:* Freight.

Cylinders (2): 19 in. × 26 in.
Boiler Pressure: 170 lb.sq.in.
Tractive Effort: 21,875 lb.
Coal Capacity: 6 tons 10 cwt.
Power Classification: 2–P/ 3–F.
Route Availability: 5.

Additional Identification Features: Slightly raised running-plate over coupled wheels.

Number Series: 64170 to 64279, with gaps due to scrapping.

Location: Seen on most lines of the Great Northern section of the Eastern Region.

* Also used for local passenger traffic.

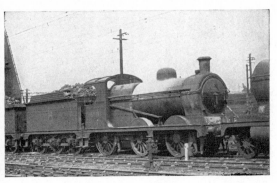

64280–64453

Origin: G.C.R.
Introduced: 1901.
Driving Wheel: 5 ft. 2 in.
*†*Weight:* 51 tons 19 cwt.
Designer: J. G. Robinson.
Purpose: Freight.

Cylinders (2): 18½ in. × 26 in.
Boiler Pressure: 180 lb.sq.in.
Tractive Effort: 21,960 lb.
Power Classification: 2-P/ 3-F.
Route Availability: 5.

Additional Identification Features: About 33 engines of this class have been rebuilt with piston valves and higher-pitched boilers, becoming reclassified "J11/3".

Number Series: 64280 to 64453 with gaps due to scrapping.

Historical Notes: Robinson's standard general purpose freight engine for the Great Central Railway. Sometimes also used on passenger trains.

Location: Seen on most parts of the former G.C.R., although not often south of Woodford. Most numerous in the Sheffield area and in Lincolnshire.

 * Tender extra: 48 tons 6 cwt. (4,000 gal.), 44 tons 3 cwt. (3,250 gal.).
 † Superheated engines weigh 3 cwt. more than the saturated ones. Some engines rebuilt from 1942 onwards with higher-pitched boilers and long-travel piston valves ("J-11/3") weigh 53 tons 6 cwt.

64460–64535

Origin: North British Railway.
Introduced: 1906.
Driving Wheel: 5 ft.
Weight: 51 tons.
Designer: W. P. Reid.
Purpose: Freight.

Cylinders (2): 18½ in. × 26 in.
Boiler Pressure: 180 lb.sq.in.
Tractive Effort: 22,080 lb.
Power Classification: 3–F.
Route Availability: 6.

Additional Identification Features: Straight footplate, with short overhang from front of smoke-box. Front splasher merged with sand-box, and rear one with cab front. Single cab windows placed well forward. Square cab side-windows.

Number Series: 64460–64535, with gaps due to scrapping.

Location: All on the former North British lines of the Scottish Region.

● Tender extra Nos. 64460-64477: 38 tons 1 cwt. Nos. 64478-64535 weigh 50 tons 15 cwt.; with tender 88 tons 10 cwt.

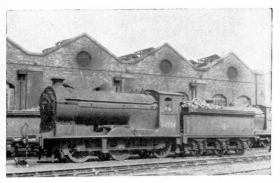

64536–64639

Origin: North British Railway.
Introduced: 1914.
Driving Wheel: 5 ft.
**Weight:* 54 tons 14 cwt.
Designer: W. P. Reid.
Purpose: Main-line Freight.

Cylinders (2): 19¼ in. × 26 in.
Boiler Pressure: 180 lb.sq.in.
Tractive Effort: 25,210 lb.
Power Classification: 5–F.
Route Availability: 8.

Additional Identification Features: A superheated edition of "J–35" class. Massive boiler with low chimney and dome. Front splasher merged with sand-box. Sloping cylinder front-cover between front of smoke-box and front buffer-beam. Shaped cab front look-outs and single side-windows. Round-topped fire-box. "J–37" has a longer footplate overhang in front of the smoke-box, a higher-pitched boiler, and shorter chimney than Class "J–35" (page 182).

Number Series: 64536 to 64639.

Location: All on the former North British lines of the Scottish Region.

* Tender extra, 40 tons 19 cwt.

64640–64674

Origin: Great Eastern Railway.
Introduced: 1912, first one re-
built Oct., 1934.
Driving Wheel: 4 ft. 11 in.
Length: 52 ft. 2 in.
Total Weight: 88 tons 12 cwt.
Designer: S. Holden.

Purpose: Freight.
Cylinders (2): 20 in. × 26 in.
Boiler Pressure: 160 and 180
lb. sq. in.
Tractive Effort: 27,430 lb.
Power Classification: 3–P/5–F.
Route Availability: 5.

Additional Identification Features: Straight footplate
with square sand-boxes between pairs of driving-wheel
splashers. All engines in this class have been rebuilt with
"D–16/3" type boiler and round-topped fire-boxes. Two
glazed windows on each side of cab.

Number Series: 64640 to 64674, with gaps due to scrapping.

Historical Notes: Nos. 64640–64649 (1912) were originally
"J–18" class (with "D–15" superheated Belpaire boilers):
Nos. 64650 to 64674 (1916–1920) were similar but with less
overhang at the front end ("J–19/1"). Nos. 64664 and
64671 have been rebuilt with smaller cylinders (19 in.) and
180 lb. sq. in. pressure, No. 64672 with 19 in. cylinders and
160 lb. pressure, whilst others with the larger cylinders
carried only 160 lb. sq. in. or 170 lb. sq. in. These alterations were responsible for variations in tractive effort
between 23,300 and 27,430 lb.

Location: All in East Anglia, on the former G.E.R. lines
of the Eastern Region.

* See Historical Notes (above).

64675–64699

Origin: G.E.R.
Introduced: 1920 and 1943.
Driving Wheel: 4 ft. 11 in.
Length: 54 ft. 6 in.
•*Weight:* 93 tons.
Water Capacity: 3,500 gals.
Designer: A. J. Hill.

Purpose: Freight.
Cylinders (2): 20 in. × 28 in.
Boiler Pressure: 180 lb.sq.in.
Tractive Effort: 29,044 lb.
Coal Capacity: 5 tons.
Power Classification: 5–F.
Route Availability: 5.

Additional Identification Features: Cab similar to "J–39" class (*q.v.*), but with longer roof as "B–12" class. Footplate slightly upswept over rear pairs of driving-wheels. Sandboxes have squared front to leading splashers and square sandboxes on footplate alongside boiler and firebox. Very short wheel-based tender.

Number Series: 64675 to 64699, with gaps due to scrapping.

Historical Notes: Engines introduced in 1920 had "B–12/1" boiler 5 ft. 1 in. diameter with Belpaire fire-box, whilst the "J–20/1" rebuilds had round-topped "B–12/3" 5 ft. 6 in. diameter boilers fitted from 1943 onwards. All the engines in this class have now been rebuilt in this way.

Location: All in East Anglia on the former G.E.R. lines of Eastern Region.

* Tender extra, 38 tons 5 cwt.

"J-39" CLASS 0-6-0

64700–64988

Origin: L.N.E.R.
Introduced: July, 1926.
Driving Wheel: 5 ft. 2 in.
Length: 55 ft. 8¾ in.
• *Weight:* 57 tons 17 cwt.
† *Water Capacity:* 4,200 gals.
Designer: Sir Nigel Gresley.

Purpose: Freight.
Cylinders (2): 20 in. × 26 in.
Boiler Pressure: 180 lb. sq. in.
Tractive Effort: 25,664 lb.
Coal Capacity: 7 tons 10 cwt.
Power Classification: 4–P/5–F.
Route Availability: 6.

Additional Identification Features: Low splashers over front two pairs of wheels: rear splashers partly enclosed by cab. Squat chimney and dome, with snifting-valve immediately behind chimney and two Ross "Pop" safety-valves mounted on top of fire-box. Cab with two windows on each side and high-pitched roof.

Number Series: 64700 to 64988, with gaps due to scrapping.

Historical Notes: A representative medium-powered goods engine of which there were 289 locomotives in the class. Various tenders were fitted (see below).

Location: Widely scattered over most parts of the Eastern and North Eastern Regions, and the former L.N.E.R. lines of the Scottish Region south of Aberdeen. Often used on passenger trains.

• Tender extra: 44 tons 4 cwt. (some, 52 tons 13 cwt.).
† Some tenders: 3,500 gal. Also various old North Eastern tenders of 3,940 or 4,125 gal.

65033–65110

Origin: North Eastern Railway.
Introduced: Sept., 1886.
Driving Wheel: 5 ft. 1¼ in.
Length: 50 ft. 8¼ in.
Total Weight: 80 tons 14 cwt.
  (superheated).
Water Capacity: 3,083 gals.
Designer: T. W. Worsdell.

Purpose: Mixed Traffic.
Cylinders (2): 19 in. × 24 in.
Boiler Pressure: 160 lb. sq. in.
Tractive Effort: 19,240 lb.
Coal Capacity: 5 tons.
Power Classification: 2–F.
Route Availability: 3.

Additional Identification Features: Straight footplate. Tall tapering chimney. Round-topped fire-box. Typical N.E.R. roomy cab, with two windows on each side and roof overhanging well to the rear. Front wheel splasher merges with sand-box, centre one is clear, and rear one merges with cab front-sheet.

Number Series: 65033, 65070, 65099, 65110.

Historical Notes: The class originally comprised 201 engines of which 171 were 2 cyl.-compounds, but all were made simples in N.E.R. days.

Location: All four survivors are in the Newcastle area.

"J–10" CLASS 0–6–0

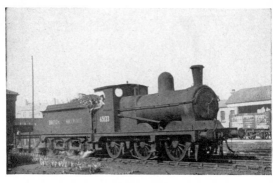

65157–65198

Origin: M.S. & L.R. and later G.C.R.
Introduced: 1892.
Designers: Parker and J. G. Robinson.
Driving Wheel: 5 ft. 1 in.

Weight: (engine only) 41 tons 6 cwt.
Cylinders: 18 in. × 26 in.
Boiler Pressure: 180 lb.sq.in.
Tractive Effort: 18,750 lb.
Power Classification: 2–F.
Route Availability: 3.

Number Series: 65157, 65192, 65198.

Historical Notes: The standard Manchester, Sheffield and Lincolnshire freight engine, perpetuated by Robinson on the Great Central until 1902.

Location: The three survivors are stationed at Wigan.

"J-36" CLASS 0–6–0

65210–65346

Origin: North British Railway.
Introduced: 1888.
Driving Wheel: 5 ft.
*Weight: 41 tons 19 cwt.
Designer: M. Holmes.
Purpose: Freight.

Cylinders (2): 18¼ in. × 26 in.
Boiler Pressure: 165 lb. sq. in.
Tractive Effort: 19,690 lb.
Power Classification: 2–F.
Route Availability: 3.

Additional Identification Features: Straight footplate.
Holmes cab originally fitted now replaced by Reid cab as
Class "J-35" and "J-37". Two of the class, Nos. 65285
and 65287, stationed at Kipps, have cut down boiler mountings including a very short stove-pipe chimney.

Number Series: 65210 to 65346, with gaps due to scrapping.

Historical Notes: 25 engines worked overseas in 1917–
1918 and were named after famous military leaders and
places connected with the First World War (see List of
Named Engines).

Location: Widely scattered over practically all sections of
the former North British lines in the Scottish Region.

* Tender extra, 33 tons 9 cwt.

189

"J-15" CLASS 0-6-0

65361–65479

Origin: Great Eastern Railway.
Introduced: July, 1883.
Driving Wheels: 4 ft. 11 in.
Length: 47 ft. 3 in.
Total Weight: 67 tons 14 cwt.
Water Capacity: 2,640 gals.
Designer: T. W. Worsdell.

Purpose: Freight and Passenger.
Cylinders: 17½ in. × 24 in.
Boiler Pressure: 160 lb. sq. in.
Tractive Effort: 16,942 lb.
Coal Capacity: 5 tons.
Power Classification: 1–P/2–F
Route Availability: 1.

Additional Identification Features: Straight footplate. Some have stove-pipe chimney and all have dome set well forward on boiler. A few have cabs with side-windows.

Number Series: 65361 to 65479, with gaps due to scrapping.

Historical Notes: A once numerous class constructed between 1883 and 1912. A useful general purpose engine which has done yeoman service on the former Great Eastern Railway for many years. Forty served overseas in 1917.

Location: The 20 or so survivors still perform much useful work in East Anglia, and despite their diminutive appearance were quite recently to be seen on passenger trains, particularly in the Cambridge and Colchester areas.

"J–17" CLASS   0–6–0

65500–65589

Origin: Great Eastern Railway.
Introduced: 1901.
Driving Wheel: 4 ft. 11 in.
*Weight: 45 tons 8 cwt.
Designer: J. Holden.
Purpose: Freight.

Cylinders (2): 19 in. × 26 in.
Boiler Pressure: 180 lb. sq. in.
Tractive Effort: 24,340 lb.
Power Classification: 2–P/4–F.
Route Availability: 4.

Additional Identification Features: Straight footplate. Low-pitched boiler, giving cab a rather large appearance. Two windows in each cab side. Front sand-box merged with front splasher and sand-boxes between front and middle splashers and between middle splasher and cab front.

Number Series: 65500 to 65589, with gaps due to scrapping.

Location: All in East Anglia on the former G.E.R. lines of the Eastern Region.

* Tender extra, 30 tons 12 cwt. or 38 tons 5 cwt., according to type fitted.

65645–65728

Origin: North Eastern Railway.	*Purpose:* Freight.
Introduced: May, 1898.	*Cylinders (2):* 18½ in. × 26 in.
Driving Wheel: 4 ft. 7¼ in.	*Boiler Pressure:* 160 lb. sq. in.
Length: 51 ft. ⅛ in.	*Tractive Effort:* 21,905 lb.
*Weight: See footnote.	*Coal Capacity:* 5 tons.
Water Capacity: 3,038 gals.	*Power Classification:* 3–F.
Designer: Wilson Worsdell.	*Route Availability:* 3.

Additional Identification Features: Very similar in appearance to "J–21" class, from which it can be distinguished most easily by its smaller splashers, and wheels. However, the front sand-boxes of "J–21's" have their fronts in line with the front of the smoke-box, whilst on the "J–25's" they are set back about 6 in.

Number Series: 65645 to 65728, with gaps due to scrapping.

Historical Notes: A mixed class, of which some engines were rebuilt with and without superheaters with consequent weight differences. Originally 120 in class, 80 built at Gateshead and 40 at Darlington (all saturated).

Location: The 15 survivors of this class are all in the North Eastern Region.

* Original design: 39 tons 11 cwt. Rebuilt with superheater: 41 tons 14 cwt. Rebuilt with superheater removed: 40 tons 17 cwt. Tender extra (in each case): 36 tons 19 cwt.

65730–65779

Origin: North Eastern Railway.
Introduced: June, 1904.
Driving Wheel: 4 ft. 7¼ in.
Length: 52 ft. 4⅛ in.
Total Weight: 83 tons 15 cwt.
Water Capacity: 3,038 gals.
Designer: Wilson Worsdell.

Purpose: Freight.
Cylinders (2): 18½ in. × 26 in.
Boiler Pressure: 180 lb.sq.in.
Tractive Effort: 24,640 lb.
Coal Capacity: 5 tons.
Power Classification: 5-F.
Route Availability: 4.

Additional Identification Features: Class "J–26" engines have class "J–25" chassis with 5 ft. 6 in. diameter boiler. Also circular windows in cab front (except where cabs have been changed over with "J–27" class).

Number Series: 65730 to 65779, with gaps due to scrapping.

Historical Notes: Thirty built at Darlington and twenty at Gateshead. Later developed into class "J–27" (*q.v.*).

Location: All in the North Eastern Region, mainly concentrated at Thornaby.

"J-27" CLASS

65780–65894

Origin: North Eastern Railway.
Introduced: April, 1906.
Driving Wheel: 4 ft. 7¼ in.
Length: 52 ft. 4⅛ in.
Total Weight: 83 tons 19 cwt. (saturated).
Water Capacity: 3,038 gals.
Designer: Wilson Worsdell.

Purpose: Freight.
Cylinders (2): 18½ in. × 26 in.
Boiler Pressure: 180 lb.sq.in.
Tractive Effort: 24,640 lb.
Coal Capacity: 5 tons.
Power Classification: 5–F.
Route Availability: 5.

Additional Identification Features: Similar to "J–26" class, but the front look-outs in the cab follow the contour of the fire-box.

Number Series: 65780 to 65894, with gaps due to scrapping.

Historical Notes: Deeper fire-box than "J–26" class. Nos. 65866–65894 (Darlington 1921–1923) of Raven's design had longer smoke-boxes, superheater and piston valves increasing the weight by 2½ tons; but in many cases the superheater has been removed (from 1943 onwards).

Location: All in the North Eastern Region.

65900–65934

Origin: L.N.E.R.
Introduced: Jan., 1926.
Driving Wheel: 4 ft. 8 in.
Total Weight: 103 tons 3 cwt.
Designer: Sir Nigel Gresley.

Cylinders: 20 in. × 26 in.
Boiler Pressure: 180 lb.sq.in.
Tractive Effort: 28,415 lb.
Power Classification: 6–F.
Route Availability: 6.

Additional Identification Features: Has a longer boiler, shorter smoke-box, and smaller driving-wheels than the "J–39" class. (See note below.) No splashers.

Number Series: 65900 to 65934.

Historical Notes: This class was a freight version of the "J–39" class (see page 186), and some engines (Nos. 65903-6-8, 65917-8, and 65926-7) have been fitted with "J–39" boilers. Designed for the Fife Coal Traffic.

Location: All in the Scottish Region, mainly in the Fife area around Dunfermline and Edinburgh.

67482–67502

Origin: North British Railway.
Introduced: 1915.
Driving Wheel: 5 ft. 9 in.
Bogie Wheel: 3 ft. 6 in.
Trailing Wheel: 3 ft. 9 in.
Length: 38 ft. 9 in.
Water Capacity: 2,080 gals.
Designer: W. P. Reid.

Purpose: Passenger.
Cylinders (2): 19 in. × 26 in.
Boiler Pressure: 165 lb.sq.in.
Tractive Effort: 19,080 lb.
Coal Capacity: 4 tons 10 cwt.
Power Classification: 2–P.
Route Availability: 6.

Number Series: 67482 to 67502, with gaps due to scrapping.

Historical Notes: The last design of suburban tank engine for the North British Railway.

Location: The last survivors of this class are in store at various N.B.R. sheds and unlikely to work again.

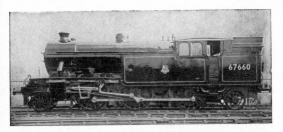

67600–67691

Origin: L.N.E.R.
Introduced: Sept., 1930.
Driving Wheel: 5 ft. 8 in.
Pony Wheel: 3 ft. 2 in.
Trailing Wheel: 3 ft. 8 in.
Length: 42 ft. ¼ in.
Weight: 86 tons 16 cwt.
Water Capacity: 2,000 gals.
Designer: Sir Nigel Gresley.

Purpose: Suburban Passenger Service.
Cylinders (3): 16 in. × 26 in.
*Boiler Pressure: 200 lb. sq. in.
*Tractive Effort: 24,960 lb.
Coal Capacity: 4 tons.
Power Classification: 4–MT.
Route Availability: 7.

Additional Identification Features: Externally the two classes are indistinguishable.

Number Series: 67600–67691.

Historical Notes: The first "V-3" engines appeared in 1939. Since then many of the original "V-1's" have been converted to "V-3".

Location: The majority of the class work the suburban services on the former L.N.E.R. lines around Glasgow and Edinburgh. A number are also on the North Eastern Region in the Newcastle and Hull districts.

* "V-1's": 180 lb. sq. in. boiler pressure; tractive effort 22,464 lb.

"L–1" CLASS

67701–67800

Origin: L.N.E.R.
Introduced: May, 1945.
Driving Wheel: 5 ft. 2 in.
Pony Wheel: 3 ft. 2 in.
Trailing Wheel: 3 ft. 2 in.
Length: 43 ft. 4 in.
Weight: 89 tons 9 cwt.
Water Capacity: 2,630 gals.

Designer: Edward Thompson.
Purpose: Mixed Traffic.
*Cylinders (2): 20 in. × 26 in.
†*Boiler Pressure:* 225 lb. sq. in.
Tractive Effort: 32,080 lb.
Coal Capacity: 4 tons 10 cwt.
Power Classification: 4–MT.
Route Availability: 7.

Additional Identification Features: Footplate raised from front buffer-beam over outside cylinders, then dropped again to buffer-beam level over middle pair of driving-wheels. Outside valve-gear. Large chimney and dome.

Number Series: 67701 to 67800.

Historical Notes: The first engine was originally numbered 9000, built at Doncaster, and painted in L.N.E.R. green: the next 29 were built at Darlington in 1948 and the remainder by contractors 1948–50.

Location: A number are used on London outer suburban services from Liverpool Street, but they are also to be found in some country areas. A few are at King's Cross for empty carriage stock working. Others are in the North Eastern Region around Darlington.

* Nos. 67770, 67771, 67772, 67776, and 67779 have 18¼-in. diameter cylinders.

† Nos. 67747 67753, 67761, 67795, and 67798 pressure reduced to 200 lb.

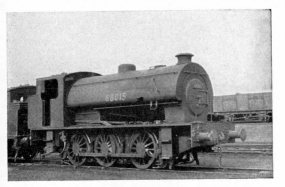

68006–68080

Origin: Ministry of Supply.
Introduced: 1946.
Driving Wheel: 4 ft. 3 in.
Weight: 48 tons 5 cwt.
Designer: R. A. Riddles, C.B.E.

Purpose: Heavy Shunting Duties.
Cylinders (2): 18 in. × 26 in.
Boiler Pressure: 170 lb.sq.in.
Tractive Effort: 23,870 lb.
Power Classification: 4–F.
Route Availability: 5.

Number Series: 68006 to 68080.

Historical Notes: Introduced during the Second World War and purchased from the Ministry of Supply in 1946. Built by Hudswell-Clarke, Bagnall, Stephenson & Hawthorns, Hunslet Eng. Co., Barclay, and Vulcan Foundry from 1944 to 1947. Several of the same class purchased by industrial concerns and the Port of London Authority; several also still owned by the W.D. Many of these work in sidings adjacent to British Railways.

Location: The majority are on the N.E. Region, but the E. Region has 25. Three are at Bidston on the L.M. Region and four others allocated to Rowsley for working on the Cromford and High Peak Railway from Middleton Top.

68095–68124

Origin: North British Railway.
Introduced: 1882.
Driving Wheel: 3 ft. 8 in.
Length: 38 ft. 2 in.
*Weight: 27 tons 16 cwt.
Designer: M. Holmes.

Purpose: Light Shunting Duties.
Cylinders (2): 14 in. × 20 in.
Boiler Pressure: 130 lb.sq.in.
Tractive Effort: 9,845 lb.
Power Classification: 0–F.
Route Availability: 2.

Additional Identification Features: Saddle-tank over boiler but not smoke-box. Tall straight-sided chimney. Outside cylinders set at slight angle to horizontal. Springs visible above footplate. Square sand-boxes over cylinders. Dumb buffers. Distinguished from Caledonian Railway "611" 0–4–0 (page 148) saddle-tanks by having a flat-topped dome, tank filler between dome and tall twin safety-valves, and stove-pipe chimney.

Number Series: 68095 to 68124, with gaps due to scrapping.

Location: At former North British sheds, chiefly in the Edinburgh and Dundee areas, with five stationed at Kipps.

   * Some engines have a wooden tender permanently attached, which weighs 6 tons.

"Y-4" CLASS 0-4-0T

33

Origin: G.E.R.
Introduced: 1913.
Designer: A. J. Hill.
Purpose: Shunting over lines
of sharp curvature.

Driving wheel: 3 ft. 10 in.
Cylinders (2): 17 in. × 20. in.
Boiler Pressure: 180 lb. sq.in.
Tractive Effort: 19,225 lb.

Additional Identification Features: Outside cylinders, Walschaerts valve-gear.

Number Series: 33 (Departmental), formerly 68129.

Historical Notes: Five of these engines, Nos. 68125–68129, were constructed, but only this one now remains. It was transferred to the Departmental list and renumbered 33 in 1952.

Location: Used as works shunter at Stratford (Old) works.

7, 21, 39, 40, 41, 42, 54, 57

Origin: Sentinel Wagon Works.
Introduced: 1925.
Driving Wheel: 2 ft. 6 in.
Weight: 20 tons 6 cwt.
Purpose: Light Dock Shunting.

Cylinders (2): 6¾ in. × 9 in.
Boiler Pressure: 275 lb. sq. in.
•Tractive Effort: (In high gear): 5,960 lb. (In low gear): 15,960 lb.
Power Classification: Unclassed.
Route Availability: 1.

Additional Identification Features: Small four-wheeled wagon-like chassis with upper works with driving cab extending two-thirds along chassis and shaped similarly to a van body.

Number Series: 7, 21, 39, 40, 41, 42, 54, 57 (formerly 68181, 68166, 68162, 68173, 68177, 68178, and 68160 in the Capital Stock).

Location: 7, Boston; 21, 42, Cambridge; 39, Norwich; 40, 41, Lowestoft; 54, 57, Darlington.

• The dimensions given apply to class "Y-3". Those of class "Y-1", which is indistinguishable in appearance, vary somewhat.

68233–68316

Origin: North Eastern Railway.
Introduced: Nov., 1886.
Driving Wheel: 4 ft. 7¼ in.
Length: 28 ft. 8¾ in.
Weight: 37 tons 12 cwt.
Water Capacity: 690 gals.
Designer: T. W. Worsdell.

Purpose : Light Freight and Station Shunting.
Cylinders (2): Various sizes.
Boiler Pressure: 140 lb. sq. in.
Tractive Effort: Various.
Coal Capacity: 1 ton 5 cwt.
Power Classification: Unclassed.
Route Availability: 1.

Additional Identification Features: Recognisable from class "J-72" by noticeably larger wheels.

Number Series: 68233/5, 68254, 68269, 68272/5/8, 68316.

Location: Scattered over the North Eastern Region, three of them being at West Auckland.

68320–68354

Origin: North British Railway.
Introduced: 1905.
Driving Wheel: 3 ft. 9 in.
Length: 26 ft. 6¾ in.
Weight: 38 tons 13 cwt.
Water Capacity: 850 gals.
Designer: W. P. Reid.

Purpose: Light Freight.
Cylinders (2): 15 in. × 22 in.
Boiler Pressure: 130 lb.sq.in.
Tractive Effort: 12,155 lb.
Coal Capacity: 2 tons 1 cwt.
Power Classification: 0–F.
Route Availability: 3.

Additional Identification Features: An engine of diminutive proportions with outside cylinders fitted with one top slide-bar.   Straight footplate.   Tall, slender, tapering chimney, small dome, and very short safety-valves mounted on a flat saddle.

Number Series: 68320 to 68354, with gaps due to scrapping.

Historical Notes: Designed with a specially short wheelbase for sharp curve negotiation during shunting operations.

Location: At former North British sheds, chiefly in the Edinburgh and Glasgow areas.

68361

Origin: N.E.R.
Introduced: 1891.
Designer: W. Worsdell.
Purpose: Shunting.

Driving Wheel: 4 ft. 7 in.
Cylinders (2): 19 in. × 24 in.
Boiler Pressure: 160 lb.sq.in.
Tractive Effort: 21,320 lb.

Additional Identification Features: A larger engine than the more numerous "J-71" and "J-72" classes of N.E.R. 0-6-0T (see pages 203 and 211).

Number Series: 68355–68364, of which only No. 68361 now remains.

Historical Notes: A series of ten engines only, constructed in 1891.

Location: The last survivor is in the Hull area.

32

Origin: G.E.R.
Introduced: 1886.
Designer: J. Holden.
Purpose: Local Freight.

Driving Wheel: 4 ft.
Cylinders: 16½ in. × 22 in.
Boiler Pressure: 160 lb.sq.in.
Tractive Effort: 16,970 lb.

Additional Identification Features: A somewhat smaller design of G.E.R. 0-6-0T than classes "J-67", "J-68" and "J-69" (pages 209 and 210).

Number Series: Departmental 32 (formerly 68370).

Historical Notes: Transferred to the Departmental list and renumbered in 1952. Now the only survivor of the class, which formerly ran from 68370 to 68388.

Location: Used as shunter at Stratford works.

68392–68410

Origin: North Eastern Railway.
Introduced: 1899.
Driving Wheel: 4 ft. 1¼ in.
Weight: 43 tons.
Designer: Wilson Worsdell.

Purpose: Light Freight and Shunting.
Cylinders (2): 17 in. × 22 in.
Boiler Pressure: 160 lb.sq.in.
Tractive Effort: 17,560 lb.
Power Classification: 2–F.
Route Availability: 2.

Additional Identification Features: Straight footplate. Springs to front pair of driving-wheels visible above footplate. Small front sand-boxes not merged with front splashers. Tall tapering chimney and large dome. Cab roof-curve carried well down sides of cab, with curved rain-strip over doorway.*

Number Series: 68392, 68408, 68410.

Historical Notes: Rebuilds of N.E.R. 0-4-4T engines designed by Edward Fletcher, and built 1874–84.

Location: Of the three survivors, one is at York, one at North Blyth, and one at West Hartlepool.

* Engines rebuilt at York have the original rounded cab-roofs, whilst those built at Darlington (e.g. No. 68392) have new square-cornered roofs.

68442–68481

Origin: North British Railway.
Introduced: 1900.
Driving Wheel: 4 ft. 6 in.
Length: 30 ft. 2¼ in.
Weight: 45 tons 5 cwt.
Water Capacity: 800 gals.
Designer: M. Holmes.

Purpose: Light Freight (and station passenger pilot duties at Waverley Stn.)*
Cylinders (2): 17 in. × 26 in.
Boiler Pressure: 150 lb.sq.in.
Tractive Effort: 17,745 lb.
Coal Capacity: 1 ton 10 cwt.
Power Classification: 2–F.
Route Availability: 4.

Additional Identification Features: Rounded top edge to tanks. Large sand-boxes combined with leading splashers.

Number Series: 68442 to 68481, with gaps due to scrapping.

Location: At former North British sheds, chiefly in the Edinburgh and Glasgow areas.

* The Waverley pilots had Westinghouse brake (later dual-fitted).

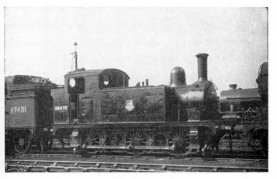

44, 45, 68490–68636

Origin: Great Eastern Railway.
Introduced: 1890–1904.
Driving Wheel: 4 ft.
Length: 27 ft. 8 in.
Weight: 40 tons.
**Water Capacity:* 1,000 and 1,140 gals.
Designer: J. Holden.
Purpose: Freight.

Cylinders (2): 16½ in. × 22 in.
**Boiler Pressure:* 160 and 180 lb. sq. in.
**Tractive Effort:* 16,970 and 19,090 lb.
Coal Capacity: 2 tons 5 cwt.
Power Classification: 2–F.
Route Availability: ("J-67") 2; ("J-69") 3.

Additional Identification Features: Distinction from "J-68" class; front end of tank top drops to lower level. Some engines have a stove-pipe chimney. No side windows to cab.

Number Series: 68490 to 68636, with gaps due to scrapping. Also on the Departmental list, 44 (late 68498), and 45 (late 68543).

Historical Notes: These two classes are almost similar in appearance, due to development and rebuilding; which resulted in varying weights, boiler pressures, and tractive efforts (see footnote). Many now have "Pop" safety-valves instead of the former encased Ramsbottom pattern.

Location: Mostly on the old G.E.R. system at Stratford and in East Anglia.

* In the two sets of figures, the first refers to "J-67" class and the second to "J-69" class (see also Historical Notes).

68642–68663

Origin: Great Eastern Railway.	*Purpose:* Freight.
Introduced: June, 1912.	*Cylinders (2):* 16½ in. × 22 in.
Driving Wheel: 4 ft.	*Boiler Pressure:* 180 lb. sq. in.
Length: 27 ft. 8 in.	*Tractive Effort:* 19,090 lb.
Weight: 42 tons 9 cwt.	*Coal Capacity:* 2 tons 10 cwt.
Water Capacity: 1,200 gals.	*Power Classification:* 2–F.
Designer: A. J. Hill.	*Route Availability:* 3.

Additional Identification Features: Short engine with straight footplate. Small-diameter boiler and high, rectangular side-tanks. Tall chimney with small dome set close behind it. Safety-valve and dome set well forward on boiler. Small bunker. Square sand-boxes on footplate alongside smoke-box. Cab side-windows, and look-outs all the same shape.

Number Series: 68642/4/6/7/9, 68650, 68660/3.

Historical Notes: The largest 0–6–0 tank engines used on the old Great Eastern Railway. Some were built expressly for passenger working.

Location: All on the G.E.R. section of the Eastern Region.

"J-72" CLASS 0–6–0T

68670–68754, 69001–69028

Origin: North Eastern Railway.
Introduced: Dec., 1898.
Driving Wheel: 4 ft. 1¼ in.
Length: 28 ft. 9¾ in.
Weight: 38 tons 12 cwt.
Water Capacity: 690 gals.
Designer: Wilson Worsdell.

Purpose: Shunting Duties.
Cylinders (2)*:* 17 in. × 24 in.
Boiler Pressure: 140 lb.sq.in.
Tractive Effort: 16,760 lb.
Coal Capacity: 2 tons.
Power Classification: 2–F
Route Availability: 2.

Additional Identification Features: Engine of small proportions. Straight footplate. Tall tapering chimney and disproportionately-large dome. Sand-box combined with front splasher. No side windows to cab.

Number Series: 68670 to 68754 and 69001 to 69028. The last 28 were not constructed until 1950–51, but were identical with the original 1898 design.

Historical Notes: The class possesses the unique record in having been built at varying periods over a span of 54 years, between 1898 and 1951, and under 3 ownerships, N.E.R., L.N.E.R. and British Railways.

Location: Mostly scattered throughout the North Eastern Region, but a few are in Scotland.

211

2, 9, 68869, 68875

Origin: G.N.R.
Introduced: 1897.
Driving Wheel: 4 ft. 8 in.
Length: 31 ft. 3¾ in.
Weight: 51 tons 41 cwt.
Water Capacity: 1,100 gals.
Designer: Stirling and Ivatt.
Purpose: Shunting Tank.

Cylinders (2): 18 in. × 26 in.
Boiler Pressure: 170 and 175 lb. sq. in.
Tractive Effort: 21,735.
Coal Capacity: 3 tons.
Power Classification: 3–F.
Route Availability: 5.

Number Series: 2, 9, 68869, 68875.

Historical Notes: Built between 1897 and 1909.

Location: Nos. 2 and 9 are works shunters at Doncaster. The other two are at Ardsley, Leeds.

68890–68991

Origin: G.N.R.
Introduced: 1922.
Driving Wheel: 4 ft. 8 in.
Length: 33 ft.
Weight: 57 tons (approx.).
Water Capacity: 1,520 gals.
Designer: Sir Nigel Gresley.

Purpose: Freight and Shunting.
Cylinders (2): 18½ in. × 26 in.
Boiler Pressure: 175 lb. sq. in.
Tractive Effort: 23,625 lb.
Coal Capacity: 4 tons 16 cwt.
Power Classification: 4–F.
Route Availability: 6.

Additional Identification Features: Side-tanks with flat top sloping down at front end.

Number Series: 68890 to 68991, with gaps due to scrapping.

Historical Notes: Some of this class were rebuilt from earlier engines built between 1913 and 1919, whilst others introduced in 1926 had minor differences from the 1922 design. Those introduced in 1937 (Nos. 68978 to 68991) were fitted with larger bunkers. Nos. 68890 to 68899 ("J–50/1") weighing 56 tons 6 cwt., and 68900 to 68919 ("J–50/2") were rebuilt from "J–51" class between 1929 and 1935.

Location: A large number are to be found at Hornsey. These work over the Metropolitan widened lines with transfer freight traffic to South London. The rest are scattered over the Eastern and North Eastern Regions, a fair number being at Ardsley. Nos. 68952 to 68958 are in the Scottish Region in the Glasgow Area.

69097–69109

Origin: North Eastern Railway.
Introduced: Oct., 1902.
Driving Wheel: 4 ft. 7¼ in.
Trailing Wheel: 3 ft. 7 in.
Weight: 57 tons 14 cwt.
Designer: Wilson Worsdell.

Purpose: Shunting.
Cylinders (2): 18½ in. × 26 in.
Boiler Pressure: 160 lb.sq.in.
Tractive Effort: 21,905 lb.
Power Classification: 3–F.
Route Availability: 3.

Number Series: 69097, 69101, 69105, 69109.

Historical Notes: A tank engine edition of the "J–25" 0–6–0 mineral engine of 1898 (see page 192).

Location: Seen on shunting duties in the Newcastle area.

"N-15" CLASS 0-6-2T

69126–69224

Origin: North British Rail-
way.
Introduced: 1910.
Driving Wheel: 4 ft. 6 in.
Trailing Wheel: 3 ft. 8 in.
*Weight: 60 tons 18 cwt.
Designer: W. P. Reid.

Purpose: Mixed Traffic and
Shunting.
Cylinders (2): 18 in × 26 in.
Boiler Pressure: 175 lb.sq.in.
Tractive Effort: 23,205 lb.
Power Classification: 3–MT
Route Availability: 6.

Number Series: 69126 to 69224, with gaps due to scrapping.

Location: Scattered throughout the former North British
lines of the Scottish Region.

* Engines Nos. 69126 to 69131 weigh 62 tons 1 cwt., and are
Class "N-15/2".

69250–69370

Origin: G.C.R.
Introduced: Aug., 1891.
Driving Wheel: 5 ft. 1 in.
Trailing Wheel: 3 ft. 6 in.
Weight: 62 tons 7 cwt.
Water Capacity: 1,400 gals.
Designer: T. Parker.

Purpose: Mixed Traffic.
Cylinders (2): 18 in. × 26 in.
Boiler Pressure: 160 lb.sq.in.
Tractive Effort: 18,780 lb.
Coal Capacity: 3½ tons.
Power Classification: 2–MT.
Route Availability: 4.

Additional Identification Features: Belpaire fireboxes and small boilers with tall domes, "flower-pot" chimneys tapering outwards.

Number Series: 69250 to 69370, with gaps due to scrapping.

Historical Notes: Developed from the Parker "N-4" class now extinct (which had Joy gear—whereas this class have link motion).

Location: Of the dozen survivors, three are at Peterborough, one at Gorton, and the remainder in the Sheffield area.

* Actually introduced on the Manchester, Sheffield and Lincolnshire Railway, the title of which was changed to Great Central Railway in 1898.

69490–69596

Origin: G.N.R.
Introduced: Nov., 1920.
Driving Wheel: 5 ft. 8 in.
Trailing Wheel: 3 ft. 8 in.
Length: 37 ft. 11½ in.
Weight: 70 tons 5 cwt. and 71 tons 9 cwt.
Water Capacity: 2,000 gals.

Designer: Sir Nigel Gresley.
Purpose: Suburban Passenger
Cylinder (2): 19 in. × 26 in.
Boiler Pressure: 170 lb. sq. in.
Tractive Effort: 19,945 lb.
Coal Capacity: 4 tons.
Power Classification: 3–P/2–F.
Route Availability: 6.

Additional Identification Features: Round-topped cab without side-windows. Condensing pipe from side of smoke-box to top of side-tank. Short vertical bridge pipe at rear end of side-tank.*

Number Series: 69490 to 69596, with gaps due to scrapping.

Historical Notes: A development of the Great Northern Railway "N–1" class. Some engines introduced in 1928 weighed slightly more than the 1925 series.

Location: Most of the class are engaged on empty stock working into Kings Cross, but a few are in the Glasgow area in the Scottish Region.

* Some engines have had their condensing gear (pipes) removed, while others were built without condensers for service in the Sc. Region.

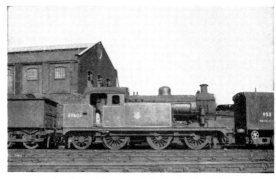

69600–69733

Origin: Great Eastern Railway.	*Designer:* A. J. Hill.
*Introduced: 1914.	*Purpose:* Suburban Passenger.
Driving Wheel: 4 ft. 10 in.	*Cylinders* (2): 18 in. × 24 in.
Trailing Wheel: 3 ft. 6 in.	*Boiler Pressure:* 180 lb. sq. in.
Length: 34 ft. 11 in.	*Tractive Effort:* 20,515 lb.
Weight: 61 tons 16 cwt. to	*Coal Capacity:* 3 tons 5 cwt.
64 tons 17 cwt.	*Power Classification:* 3–MT.
Water Capacity: 1,600 gals.	*Route Availability:* 5.

Number Series: 69600 to 69733, with gaps due to scrapping.

Historical Notes: The first two engines entered regular service in 1915, though dated 1914. Ten more were built in 1921. Others appeared in 1925 and 1926, while a series with round-topped fireboxes were built at Doncaster in 1927. More round-topped fireboxes appeared on rebuilds in 1940 and 1943, and all the class now carry round-topped boilers.

Location: The vast majority of the class are based at Stratford and work the remaining steam-operated suburban services out of Liverpool Street. A few have been drafted to country districts and there is a small allocation at Hatfield.

*See Historical Notes (above).

"A-5" CLASS

4-6-2T

69800–69842

Origin: G.C.R.
Introduced: March, 1911.
Driving Wheel: 5 ft. 7 in.
Bogie Wheel: 3 ft. 6 in.
Trailing Wheel: 3 ft. 9 in.
Length: 42 ft. 11⅞ in.
★ Total Weight: 85 tons 18 cwt.
Water Capacity: 2,280 gals.

Designer: J. G. Robinson.
Purpose: Suburban Passenger.
Cylinders (2): 20 in. × 26 in.
Boiler Pressure: 180 lb. sq. in.
Tractive Effort: 23,743 lb.
Coal Capacity: 4 tons 3 cwt.
Power Classification: 3–MT.
Route Availability: 5.

Additional Identification Features: Inside cylinders.
Cab fitted with two windows on each side.

Number Series: Introduced in 1911: 69800 to 69829
("A–5/1"). Added in 1925: 69830 to 69842 ("A–5/2")
for N.E. Area. All of the last mentioned are now scrapped,
and only four of the earlier ones remain.

Historical Notes: This class was perpetuated after the Great
Central Railway became merged with other companies to
form the L.N.E.R., and in 1925 appeared the modifications
of boiler mountings noticeable on engines Nos. 69830 to
69842.

Location: The survivors of the class work in the Lincolnshire district.

★ Engines added in 1925 weighed 90 tons 11 cwt.

69850–69894

Origin: North Eastern Railway.
*Introduced: 1913.
Driving Wheel: 5 ft. 9 in.
Bogie Wheel: 3 ft. 1¼ in.
Trailing Wheel: 3 ft. 9 in.
Length: 42 ft. 6¼ in.
Total Weight: 86 tons 18 cwt.
Water Capacity: 2,000 gals.

Designer: Sir Vincent Raven.
Purpose: Passenger.
Cylinders (3): 16½ in. × 26 in.
Boiler Pressure: 175 lb.sq.in.
Tractive Effort: 22,940 lb.
Coal Capacity: 4 tons.
Power Classification: 3–MT.
Route Availability: 5.

Additional Identification Features: Easily distinguishable from class "A–5" by having outside cylinders. High-built bunker with vertically arranged coal-rails.

Number Series: 69850 to 69894, with gaps due to scrapping.

Historical Notes: These engines were rebuilt by Sir Nigel Gresley in 1931 from the old North Eastern "D" class of 4-4-4T type (L.N.E.R. Class "H-1").

Location: All in the N.E. Region.

* See Historical Notes (above).

69921

Origin: N.E.R.
Introduced: 1909.
Designer: W. Worsdell.
Purpose: Heavy Shunting.

Driving Wheel: 4 ft. 7¼ in.
Cylinders (3): 18 in. × 26 in.
Boiler Pressure: 175 lb. sq.in.
Tractive Effort: 34,080.

Additional Identification Features: A rare type of wheel arrangement, 4–8–0T, the only other engines being on the S.R. (page 69).

Number Series: 69921.

Historical Notes: Ten engines were originally built in 1909, and another five added by Sir Nigel Gresley in 1925.

Location: The last survivor of the class is shedded at Tyne Dock.

70000–70054

Introduced: 1951
Driving Wheel: 6 ft. 2 in.
Bogie Wheel: 3 ft.
Trailing Wheel: 3 ft. 3½ in.
Length: 68 ft. 9 in.
Weight: (Loco) 94 tons.
   (Tender) Type BR 1
   47 tons 4 cwt; Type
   BR 1E, 55 tons 10 cwt.

Water Capacity: BR 1 type,
   4,250 gals.
Purpose: Mixed Traffic.
Cylinders: 20 in. × 28 in.
Boiler Pressure: 250 lb. sq. in.
Tractive Effort: 32,150 lb.
Coal Capacity: 7 tons.
Power Classification: 7–MT.
Route Availability: 8.

Number Series: 70000 to 70054.

Historical Notes: This, the first of the twelve new British Railway types to appear, was designed at Derby and built at Crewe, sections being designed at Brighton, Doncaster and Swindon, all being under the direction of R. A. Riddles.
   No. 70004 was exhibited at the Festival of Britain; Nos. 70045–70054 have curved-sided tenders (Class BR 1E).

Location: 70000–70003, 70005–70013, 70030 and 70034–70041 work on the E.R. main lines between Liverpool Street and Norwich. The others are divided between the Midland, Western, North Eastern and Scottish Regions.

4-6-2

71000

Introduced: 1954.
Driving Wheel: 6 ft. 2 in.
Bogie Wheel: 3 ft.
Trailing Wheel: 3 ft. 3½ in.
Length: 70 ft.
Weight:
  (Engine) 101 tons 5 cwt.
  (Tender) 55 tons 10 cwt.

Water Capacity: 4,725 gals.
Purpose: Express Passenger.
Cylinders (3): 18 in. × 28 in.
Boiler Pressure: 250 lb. sq. in.
Tractive Effort: 39,080 lb.
Coal Capacity: 10 tons.
Power Classification: 8–P.

Additional Identification Features: By number, British-Caprotti valve-gear and double chimney.

Number: 71000 ("Duke of Gloucester").

Historical Notes: Designed at Derby. Completed at the Crewe Works of the London Midland Region in 1954, No. 71000 was named by permission of H.R.H. the Duke of Gloucester, in commemoration of the Duke's Honorary Presidency of the International Railway Congress which was held in London on May 19–26, 1954.

    The locomotive is designed for hauling the heaviest and fastest express passenger services, and is more powerful than the "Britannia" Class and other B.R. standard engines. Unfortunately, owing to the decision to cease construction of steam locomotives, no more of this class will now appear.

Location: Stationed at Crewe, and works over the West Coast main line of the L.M. Region.

223

72000—72009

Introduced: 1951.
Driving Wheel: 6 ft. 2 in.
Bogie Wheel: 3 ft.
Trailing Wheel: 3 ft. 3½ in.
Length: 68 ft. 9 in.
Weight:
  (Loco) 86 tons 19 cwt.
  (Tender) Type BR1,
    47 tons 4 cwt.

Water Capacity: 4,250 gals.
Purpose: Mixed Traffic.
Cylinders: 19½ in. × 28 in.
Boiler Pressure: 225 lb. sq.
  in.
Tractive Effort: 27,520 lb.
Coal Capacity: 7 tons.
Power Classification: 6—MT.
Route Availability: 7.

Additional Identification Features: High running-plate and smaller diameter boiler, taller dome and chimney than Class "7—MT" 4—6—2; also "Clan" names.

Number Series: 72000 to 72009.

Historical Notes: Designed at Derby and built at Crewe, the engines of this class were constructed for service in the Scottish Region.

Location: Nos. 72000—4 at Polmadie (Glasgow) and 72005 at Carlisle (Kingmoor). Not regularly seen south of Crewe.

* R.A. 8 with 5,000-gal. tender.

4-6-0

73000–73171

Introduced: April, 1951.
Driving Wheel: 6 ft. 2 in.
Bogie Wheel: 3 ft.
Length: 62 ft. 7 in.
Weight:
  (Loco) 76 tons 4 cwt.
  (Tender) Type BR 1 as illustrated, 47 tons 4 cwt. Type BR 1 G on a few engines, 52½ tons.

Water Capacity: 4,250 gals.
Purpose: Mixed Traffic.
Cylinders: 19 in. × 28 in.
Boiler Pressure: 225 lb.sq.in.
Tractive Effort: 26,120 lb.
Coal Capacity: 7 tons.
Power Classification: 5—MT.
Route Availability: 7.

Additional Identification Features: Most easily identified by whistle behind chimney and wheels which reach almost up to running-plate. Nos. 73125–73154 have Caprotti valve-gear.

Number Series: 73000 to 73171.

Historical Notes: The first of this class was completed at Derby in April, 1951, having been designed and built under the direction of Mr. R. A. Riddles, Railway Executive Member for Mechanical and Electrical Engineering.
  A direct development of the well-known L.M.S. Class "5" mixed traffic engines (page 123).

Location: On the main lines of all the Regions, although comparatively rare on the Eastern.

4-6-0

75000–75079

Introduced: May, 1951.
Driving Wheel: 5 ft. 8 in.
Bogie Wheel: 3 ft.
Length: 50 ft.
Weight:
   (Loco) 69 tons.
   (Tender) 43 tons 3 cwt.
Water Capacity: 3,500 gals.

Purpose: Mixed Traffic.
Cylinders: 18 in. × 28 in.
Boiler Pressure: 225 lb sq.in.
Tractive Effort: 25,100 lb.
Coal Capacity: 6 tons.
Power Classification: 4—MT.
* *Route Availability:* 4.

Additional Identification Features: Smaller boiler than B.R. Class "5" (Page 225), this being very noticeable from front end. Also smaller wheels. Some of the class are being fitted with double chimneys.

Number Series: 75000 to 75079.

Historical Notes: This was the smaller of the two 4-6-0 mixed traffic locomotives among the six British Railway types built at Swindon in 1951 under the direction of Mr. R. A. Riddles. The parent office for design was Brighton, although certain parts were designed at Swindon, Doncaster and Derby. Similar in many respects to the British Railways Class "5", the "75000's" are lighter engines, having almost universal availability over main and secondary lines throughout Britain. The boiler follows closely the design of that of the L.M.R. Class "4" 2-6-4T engines, except that the barrel is some nine inches longer.

Location: Divided between the Midland, Western and Southern Regions.

* With 5,000-gal. tender, R.A. 7.

2-6-0

76000–76114

Introduced: Dec., 1952.
Driving Wheels: 5 ft. 3 in.
Pony Wheel: 3 ft.
Length: 55 ft. 10½ in.
Weight:
  (Loco) 59 tons 2 cwt.
  (Tender) 42 tons 3 cwt.
Water Capacity: 3,500 gals.

Purpose: Mixed Traffic.
Cylinders: 17½ in. × 26 in.
Boiler Pressure: 225 lb. sq. in.
Tractive Effort: 24,170 lb.
Coal Capacity: 6 tons.
Power Classification: 4–MT.
Route Availability: 4.

Additional Identification Features: Raised footplate, cylinders set at sharp angle to horizontal. Cab closed at rear by built-up tender.

Number Series: 76000 to 76114.

Historical Notes: Designed at Doncaster and built at Horwich and Doncaster. Developed from Ivatt "43000" class (page 119).

    The low axle loading of under 17 tons of this class gives it a wide Route Availability. It was designed to attain maximum interchangeability with other B.R. standard types in all its details, and by this means maintenance is facilitated.

Location: Divided amongst all except the Western Regions, the largest allocations being to the Southern and the Scottish.

2-6-0

77000–77019

Introduced: Feb., 1954.
Driving Wheel: 5 ft. 3 in.
Pony Wheel: 3 ft.
Length: 55 ft. 11¼ in.
Weight:
    (Loco) 57 tons 9 cwt.
    (Tender) Class BR–2A
    42 tons 3 cwt.

Water Capacity: 3,500 gals
Purpose: Mixed Traffic.
Cylinders: 17½ in. × 26 in.
Boiler Pressure: 200 lb.sq.in.
Tractive Effort: 21,490 lb.
Coal Capacity: 6 tons.
Power Classification: 3–MT.

Additional Identification Features: The high running-plate is particularly accentuated in this class by the small driving wheels, resulting in a very ugly engine.

Number Series: 77000 to 77019.

Historical Notes: Built at Swindon. First appeared in February, 1954. Designed for working on almost any main or secondary lines throughout Britain.

Location: Divided evenly between the North Eastern and Scottish Regions. They are never seen in the south of England.

2–6–0

78000–78064

Introduced: Dec., 1952.
Driving Wheel: 5 ft.
Pony Wheel: 3 ft.
Length: 53 ft. 2¼ in.
Weight:
  (Loco) 49 tons 5 cwt.
  (Tender) 36 tons 17 cwt.
Water Capacity: 3,000 gals.

Purpose: Mixed Traffic.
Cylinders: 16½ in. × 24 in.
Boiler Pressure: 200 lb.sq.in.
Tractive Effort: 18,515 lb.
Coal Capacity: 4 tons.
Power Classification: 2–MT.
Route Availability: 3.

Additional Identification Features: Resembles L.M.S. Class (page 130).

Number Series: 78000 to 78064.

Historical Notes: Built at Darlington under the direction of R. A. Riddles, and was directly derived from Mr. Ivatt's "46400" class of the L.M.S. This is the smallest of the B.R. standard types and, amongst the tender classes, alone possesses a running-plate of moderate height, resulting in the best proportioned engine of all the new designs.

Location: Divided amongst all Regions except the Southern.

2-6-4T

80000–80154

Introduced: July, 1951.
Driving Wheel: 5 ft. 8 in.
Pony Wheel: 3 ft.
Trailing Wheel: 3 ft.
Length: 44 ft. 9⅝ in.
Weight: 86 tons 13 cwt.
Water Capacity: 2,000 gals.
Purpose: Mixed Traffic.

Cylinders: 18 in. × 28 in.
Boiler Pressure: 225 lb. sq. in.
Tractive Effort: 25,100 lb.
Coal Capacity: 3½ tons.
Power Classification: 4–MT, 4–P/4–F on Southern Region.
Route Availability: 5.

Additional Identification Features: Tank sides slope inwards, as do cab and bunkers, to conform to loading gauge requirements.

Number Series: 80000 to 80154.

Historical Notes: The first locomotives of this class (Nos. 80010–80053) were built at Brighton Works, whilst Nos. 80000–80009 and 80045–80058 were constructed at Derby L.M.R. and Nos. 80106–80115 at Doncaster, Brighton continuing with Nos. 80116–80154.

The engines were designed and built under the supervision of Mr. R. A. Riddles, and were a direct derivation of the Stanier and Fairburn engines of the L.M.S. (see page 114), which were in turn developed from Sir Henry Fowler's 1927 design (page 115).

Location: Particularly numerous on the former L.B. & S.C.R. and L.T. & S.R. lines, and in the Glasgow area. Five others are at Leeds, but there are now none on the L.M. or Western Regions.

2-6-2T

82000–82044

Introduced: April, 1952.
Driving Wheel: 5 ft. 3 in.
Pony Wheel: 3 ft.
Trailing Wheel: 3 ft.
Length: 40 ft. 10½ in.
Weight: 74 tons 1 cwt.
Water Capacity: 1,500 gals.

Purpose: Light Passenger.
Cylinders: 17½ in. × 26 in.
Boiler Pressure: 200 lb.sq.in.
Tractive Effort: 21,490 lb.
Coal Capacity: 3 tons.
Power Classification: 3–MT.
Route Availability: 4.

Additional Identification Features: Straight tank top, cut away below, over motion. Boiler sharply tapered.

Number Series: 82000 to 82044.

Historical Notes: Designed at Swindon, this class offers an engine in power and axle-loading half-way between the class 4–MT tender and class 2–MT tank engines. The boiler is virtually a Swindon "No. 2", modified to carry a dome and normal type of superheater. Otherwise this class was for the most part a new design.

Location: The majority of the class are on the Western Region. The Southern also has a number: a few are found in the North-Eastern Region and also around Chester.

2-6-2T

84000–84029

Introduced: July, 1953.
Driving Wheel: 5 ft.
Pony Wheel: 3 ft.
Trailing Wheel: 3 ft.
Length: 38 ft. 9½ in.
Weight: 63 tons 5 cwt.
Water Capacity: 1,350 gals.

Purpose: Mixed Traffic.
Cylinders: 16½ in. × 24 in.
Boiler Pressure: 200 lb.sq.in.
Tractive Effort: 18,515 lb.
Coal Capacity: 3 tons.
Power Classification: 2–MT.
Route Availability: 1.

Additional Identification Features: A distinctly smaller engine than the 82000 class. All are motor fitted for pull and push working.

Number Series: 84000 to 84029.

Historical Notes: Designed at Derby, under the overall direction of Mr. R. A. Riddles, and was directly derived from Ivatt's "41200" class on the L.M.S. (see page 108).

Location: 84000–84019 all on the Midland Region, chiefly engaged on branch lines. 84020–84029 are on the Southern, in East Kent.

90000–90732

Origin: Ministry of Supply.
Introduced: Feb., 1943.
Driving Wheel: 4 ft. 8½ in.
Pony Wheel: 3 ft. 2 in.
Length: 63 ft. 6 in.
Weight:
   (Loco) 70 tons 5 cwt.
   (Tender) 55 tons 10 cwt.
Water Capacity: 5,000 gals.

Designer: R. A. Riddles, C.B.E.
Purpose: Long-distance
   Freight.
Cylinders: 19 in. × 28 in.
Boiler Pressure: 225 lb. sq. in.
Tractive Effort: 34,215 lb.
Coal Capacity: 9 tons.
Power Classification: 8-F.
Route Availability: 6.

Number Series: 90000 to 90732.

Historical Notes: "Austerity" engines built to Ministry of Supply design. 200 (which with others of the class had been on loan from the War Dept.) were purchased by the L.N.E.R. in December, 1946, and numbered 3000 to 3199. Nos. 3000 to 3100 were built by the North British Locomotive Co. Ltd, and 3101 to 3199 by the Vulcan Foundry Ltd. In 1948, British Railways added 60000 to these numbers. When 533 more engines of the same class were taken over by British Railways early in 1949 the North British-built locomotives were numbered 90000 to 90421, and the Vulcan Foundry locomotives followed on as 90422 to 90732 in approximate order of date of construction—except that 63000 to 63100 became 90000 to 90100, and 63101 to 63199 became 90422 to 90520. Engine No. 90732 is named "Vulcan" high up on the cab side.

Location: This numerous class is found on the main lines of all Regions except the Southern.

233

90750–90774

Origin: Ministry of Supply.
Introduced: 1943.
Driving Wheel: 4 ft. 8½ in.
Pony Wheel: 3 ft. 2 in.
Length: 67 ft. 6¼ in.
Weight:
    (Loco) 78 tons 6 cwt.
    (Tender) 55 tons 10 cwt.
Water Capacity: 5,000 gals.

Designer: R. A. Riddles, C.B.E.
Purpose: Long-distance Freight.
Cylinders: 19 in. × 28 in.
Boiler Pressure: 225 lb. sq. in.
Tractive Effort: 34,215 lb.
Coal Capacity: 9 tons.
Power Classification: 8–F.

Additional Identification Features: Most easily identified by Number Series (*q.v.*). The unusual chimney is similar to that used on the 2–8–0 "W.D." class (page 233).

Number Series: 90750 to 90774.

Historical Notes: These are the "Austerity" engines built to Ministry of Supply design and purchased by British Railways in December, 1948, after being worked "on loan" for some time, as a new type of special heavy traffic locomotive. They were designed at Crewe, built by the North British Locomotive Co. Ltd, and intended principally for working mineral traffic. They embody features common to other British Railway Standard types.

Location: All working in Scotland.

2–10–0

92000–92250

Introduced: 1954.
Driving Wheel: 5 ft.
Pony Wheel: 3 ft. 2 in.
Length: 66 ft. 2 in.
Weight:
  (Loco) 86 tons 14 cwt.
  * (Tender) 53 tons 10 cwt.
Water Capacity: varies.

Purpose: Heavy Mineral
  Freight.
Cylinders (2): 20 in. × 28 in.
Boiler Pressure: 250 lb. sq. in.
Tractive Effort: 39,667 lb.
Coal Capacity: varies.
Power Classification: 9–F.

Additional Identification Features: British Railways Standard freight engine. Note high running-plate, broad fire-box, and inclined cylinders. Some of the later ones have double chimneys and No. 92220 a copper-capped chimney in G.W.R. style.

Number Series: 92000–92250.

Historical Notes: The last of the twelve standard designs produced by B.R. before going over to Diesel traction. No. 92220 was the final one built, being turned out from Swindon in March 1960. Named "Evening Star" in commemoration of being the last new steam locomotive constructed for British Railways.

Location: Seen on heavy mineral trains on the L.M., E., N.E. and W. Regions. No. 92079 is stationed at Bromsgrove and banks on the Lickey incline.

   * Tender weight varies. 52 tons 10 cwt. for first series with BR 1G tender. Nos. 92010–92014 have BR 1F tenders weighing 55 tons 10 cwt.

"FRANCO-CROSTI" CLASS 2–10–0

92020–92029

Introduced: 1955.
Driving Wheel: 5 ft.
Pony Wheel: 3 ft. 2 in.
Length: 66 ft. 2 in.
Weight:
   (Loco.) 86 tons 14 cwt.
   (Tender) 53 tons 10 cwt.
Water Capacity: varies.

Purpose: Heavy Mineral
  Freight.
Cylinders (2): 20 in. × 28 in.
Boiler Pressure: 250 lb.sq.in.
Tractive Effort: 39,667 lb.
Coal Capacity: varies.
Power Classification: 9–F.

Additional Identification Features: A variation of the B.R. standard 2–10–0 (previous page). Distinguished by the peculiar Franco-Crosti double-barrelled boiler and also, when in steam, by the exhaust being emitted from a chimney half-way along the right-hand side of the boiler. The chimney in the normal place on the smokebox is only used for lighting up when the engine is being steamed. These boilers are now being replaced by the normal type.

Number Series: 92020 to 92029.

Location: All stationed at Wellingborough and work freight trains on the Midland Division main line, principally to Cricklewood.

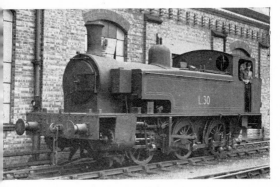

L30, L31

Origin: District Railway.
Introduced: 1931.
Driving Wheel: 4 ft. 3 in.

Cylinders: 16 in. × 24 in.
Boiler Pressure: 200 lb. sq. in.

Number Series: L30, L31.

Historical Notes: Built by the Hunslet Engine Co. in 1931 for shunting at the District Railway's Lillie Bridge depot. Absorbed into London Transport stock in 1933.

Location: Still usually to be found at Lillie Bridge.

L44, L46, L48

Origin: Metropolitan Railway.
Introduced: 1896.
Driving Wheel: 5 ft. 6 in.

Cylinders: $17\frac{1}{2}$ in. $\times$ 26 in.
Boiler Pressure: 150 lb. sq. in.
Tractive Effort: 15,320 lb.

Number Series: L44, L46, L48 (formerly Metropolitan Nos. 1, 77 and 81).

Historical Notes: Survivors of a series of seven engines built by the Metropolitan Railway between 1896 and 1901. Formerly used for passenger working over the non-electrified section of the line beyond Harrow (later Rickmansworth).

Location: Now to be found at Neasden on local freight and shunting work.

L52

Origin: Metropolitan Railway.
Introduced: 1901.
Driving Wheel: 5 ft. 2 in.

Cylinders: 17½ in. × 26 in.
Boiler Pressure: 150 lb.
Tractive Effort: 16,350 lb.

Number Series: L52 (formerly Metopolitan No. 93).

Historical Notes: Survivor of a class of four engines built in 1901 for freight work.

Location: Now to be found at Neasden on local freight and shunting work.

METROPOLITAN RAILWAY

PECKETT 0–6–0ST

L53, L54

Origin: Metropolitan Railway.
Introduced: 1897.
Driving Wheels: 3 ft. 10 in.

Cylinders: 16 in. × 22 in.
Boiler Pressure: 140 lb. sq. in.
Tractive Effort: 14,520 lb.

Number Series: L53, L54 (formerly Metropolitan 101, 102).

Historical Notes: Two engines of standard Peckett design built for the Metropolitan Railway for general shunting duties.

Location: One usually to be found at Neasden and one at Lillie Bridge.

L90–L94

Origin: G.W.R.
Introduced: 1929.
Driving Wheel: 4 ft. 7½ in.
Cylinder: 17½ in. × 24 in.

Boiler Pressure: 200 lb. sq. in.
Tractive Effort: 22,515 lb.

Number Series: L90–L94 (late B.R. 7711, 5752, 5786, 7779, and 7752).

Historical Notes: Standard G.W.R. 0–6–0 PT's purchased from British Railways between 1956 and 1959 to replace older Metropolitan engines on shunting duties.

Location: Allocated to Neasden depot.

1–18

Origin: Metropolitan Railway.
Introduced: 1922.

Weight: 56 tons.
Tractive Effort: 1,200 h.p.
Type: Bo-Bo.

Number Series: 1–14, 16, 18.

Historical Notes: These engines were reconstructions of two earlier series, Nos. 1–10, which had been built in 1904, and 11–20, turned out in 1906. Nos. 15, 17, 19, and 20 have been scrapped. All carry names.

Location: Based on Neasden, these engines work the through Aylesbury line trains between Rickmansworth and Baker Street or Liverpool Street.

B.R. ELECTRIC LOCOMOTIVES

Running numbers	Type	Class	Tractive effort lb.	Origin and other particulars	Location
20001, 20002	Co–Co	CC	40,000	Bulleid/Raworth S.R. design, 1941. 3rd rail current collection	On S.R. Brighton electrified section
20003	Co–Co	CC	45,000	Development of above, 1948	On S.R. Brighton electrified section
26000 to 26057	Bo–Bo	EM1	45,000	Gresley/Metro-Vickers, 1941 (No. 26000, now named "Tommy") 1950. Overhead current collection	On Manchester–Sheffield–Wath electrified lines
26500, 26501	Bo–Bo	ES1	25,000	Brush / Thompson - Houston N.E.R. design, 1902. 3rd rail and overhead current collection	On Quayside branch, Newcastle working from Gosforth shed
D100	Bo–Bo	EB1	37,600	L.N.E.R. rebuild of Raven 1914 design for N.E.R. Overhead current collection	Shunts at Ilford carriage sidings
27000 to 27006	Co–Co	EM2	45,000	L.N.E.R./Metro-Vickers 1954 design	On Manchester–Sheffield–Wath electrified lines
E2001	A1A–A1A	—	40,000	Rebuilt from Gas Turbine loco 18100	—
E5000 to E5023	Bo–Bo	—	43,000	3rd Rail and Overhead	S.R.

Some new series of electric locomotives are now under construction for use on the forthcoming Manchester–Crewe and Liverpool–Crewe electrification schemes (eventually to be extended south to Euston). These will be numbered in two series from E3001 and E3301 upwards.

ELECTRIC LOCOMOTIVES

Class CC, No. 20002, type Co–Co

Class EM1, No. 26035, type Bo–Bo

Class EM2, No. 27001 "Ariadne", type Co–Co

B.R. DIESEL LOCOMOTIVES

Running numbers*	Type	Classification†	Builders and Type of Engine	Tractive Effort (lb.)
D1 –D147	1 Co-Co 1	DE	B.R./Sulzer	70,000
D200 –D304	1 Co-Co 1	DE	English Electric	52,000
D600 –D604	A1A–A1A	DH	North British Loco. Co.	50,000
D800 –D865	B–B	DH	Swindon/Maybach	52,400
D1500–D1521‡	Co–Co	DE	English Electric (Deltic)	—
D2000–D2174	0-6-0	DM	B.R./Gardner	15,650
D2200–D2295	0-6-0	DM	Drewry/Gardner	16,850
D2400–D2409	0-4-0	DM	Barclay/Gardner	15,340
D2410–D2444	0-4-0	DM	Barclay/Gardner	20,000
D2500–D2509	0-6-0	DM	Hudswell Clarke/Gardner	16,100
D2550–D2618	0-6-0	DM	Hunslet/Gardner	14,500

* Under the original British Railways numbering scheme it was intended that all Diesel locomotives should be numbered in the series 10000–19999. This plan, however, has recently been modified, and all newer types of diesels are now being numbered in a separate series prefixed by the letter D. As construction of these new engines is proceeding apace and will continue to do so, the numbers of the individual engines are given as far as is known at the time of going to press, but in many cases it may be some time before all are actually constructed, whilst other new series may appear, the details of which have not yet been announced.

A number of the earlier classes of Diesel locomotives of pre-nationalisation design are not being renumbered. They are in the 10000, 12000 and 15000 series, and these will continue to carry their old numbers.

There are also sundry Departmental locomotives which are not numbered in any particular series. As these are very seldom seen and only of minor interest, they are not detailed.

On pages 245–247 will be found tabulated particulars of the number series, etc., of the various classes of Diesel locomotives, followed by illustrations of the principal varieties. Considerations of space, however, will not allow every class to be illustrated.

† DE—Diesel Electric. DM—Diesel Mechanical. DH—Diesel Hydraulic.

‡ Not yet constructed. These numbers may be changed to D9000–D9021.

Running numbers	Type	Classification	Builders and Type of Engine	Tractive Effort (lb.)
D2700–D2707	0-4-0	DH	North British Loco Co./ Paxman	21,500
D2708–D2779	0-4-0	DH	North British Loco. Co.	20,080
D2900–D2920	0-4-0	DH	North British Loco. Co.	24,100
D2950–D2952	0-4-0	DM	Hunslet/Gardner	10,800
D2953–D2956	0-4-0	DM	Barclay/Gardner	12,750
D2957, D2958	0-4-0	DM	Ruston and Hornsby	14,350
D3000–D3116	0-6-0	DE	B.R./English Electric	35,000
D3117–D3126	0-6-0	DE	B.R./Crossley	35,000
D3127–D3136	0-6-0	DE	B.R./English Electric	35,000
D3137–D3166	0-6-0	DE	B.R./Blackstone	35,000
D3167–D3438	0-6-0	DE	B.R./English Electric	35,000
D3439–D3453	0-6-0	DE	B.R./Blackstone	35,000
D3454–D3472	0-6-0	DE	B.R./English Electric	35,000
D3473–D3502	0-6-0	DE	B.R./Blackstone	35,000
D3503–D3611	0-6-0	DE	B.R./English Electric	35,000
D3612–D3651	0-6-0	DE	B.R./Blackstone	35,000
D3652–D4094	0-6-0	DE	B.R./English Electric	35,000
D5000–D5150	Bo–Bo	DE	B.R./Sulzer	40,000
D5300–D5346	Bo–Bo	DE	Birmingham C. & W. Co./Sulzer	42,000
D5500–D5699*	A1A–A1A	DE	Brush	42,000
D5700–D5719	Co–Bo	DE	Met. Vickers/Crossley	50,000
D5900–D5909	Bo–Bo	DE	English Electric	47,000
D6100–D6157	Bo–Bo	DE	North British Loco. Co.	45,000
D6300–D6357	B–B	DE	North British Loco. Co.	40,000

* This class will probably be continued from D5800 onwards.

Running numbers	Type	Classification	Builders and Type of Engine	Tractive Effort (lb.)
D6500–D6576	Bo–Bo	DE	Birmingham C. & W. Co./Sulzer	45,000
D8000–D8049	Bo–Bo	DE	Vulcan Foundry/English Electric	42,000
D8200–D8236	Bo–Bo	DE	British Thomson-Houston Co./Paxman	37,500
D8400–D8409	Bo–Bo	DE	North British Loco. Co./Paxman	42,000
10000, 10001	Co–Co	DE	Derby/English Electric	41,400
10201, 10202	1 Co–Co 1	DE	Ashford/English Electric	48,000
10203	1 Co–Co 1	DE	Ashford/English Electric	50,000
12000, 12001	0–6–0	DE	English Electric	30,000
12003–12032	0–6–0	DE	Derby/English Electric	33,000
12033–12138	0–6–0	DE	Derby/English Electric	35,000
15000–15003	0–6–0	DE	Doncaster/English Electric	32,000
15004	0–6–0	DE	Doncaster/Petter	32,000
15100	0–6–0	DE	English Electric	30,000
15101–15106	0–6–0	DE	Swindon/English Electric	33,500
15201–15203	0–6–0	DE	Ashford/English Electirc	30,000
15211–15236	0–6–0	DE	Ashford/English Electric	24,000

GAS TURBINE LOCOMOTIVE

Running number	Type	Classification	Builders and Type of Engine	Tractive Effort (lb.)
18000	A1A–A1A	—	Swiss Loco. & Machine Works, Winterthur Brown-Boveri	60,000

DIESEL LOCOMOTIVES

Diesel electric locomotive No. D3 "Skiddaw",
type Co–Co 1

Diesel electric locomotive No. D265,
type 1 Co–Co 1

DIESEL LOCOMOTIVES

Diesel hydraulic locomotive No. D600
"Active", type A1A–A1A

Diesel hydraulic locomotive No. D800
" Sir Brian Robertson", type B–B

DIESEL LOCOMOTIVES

Diesel mechanical locomotive No. D2085,
type 0–6–0

Diesel mechanical locomotive No. D2275,
type 0–6–0

DIESEL LOCOMOTIVES

Diesel mechanical locomotive No. D2420,
type 0–4–0

Diesel mechanical locomotive No. D2582,
type 0–6–0

DIESEL LOCOMOTIVES

Diesel hydraulic locomotive No. D2705,
type 0–4–0

Diesel hydraulic locomotive No. D2720,
type 0–4–0

DIESEL LOCOMOTIVES

Diesel electric locomotive No. D3016,
type o–6–o

Diesel electric locomotive No. D5022,
type Bo–Bo

DIESEL LOCOMOTIVES

Diesel electric locomotive No. D5344,
type Bo–Bo

Diesel electric locomotive No. D5588,
type A1A–A1A

DIESEL LOCOMOTIVES

Diesel electric locomotive No. D5718,
type Co–Bo

Diesel electric locomotive No. D5905,
type Bo–Bo

DIESEL LOCOMOTIVES

Diesel electric locomotive No. D6143,
type Bo–Bo

Diesel electric locomotive No. D8014,
type Bo–Bo

DIESEL LOCOMOTIVES

Diesel electric locomotive No. D8202,
type Bo–Bo

Diesel electric locomotive No. 10000,
type Co–Co

DIESEL LOCOMOTIVES

Diesel electric locomotive No. D10202,
type 1 Co–Co 1

Diesel electric locomotive No. D12028.
type 0–6–0

DIESEL LOCOMOTIVE

Diesel electric locomotive No. 15235,
type o–6–o

GAS TURBINE LOCOMOTIVE

No. 18000, type AIA–AIA

ALPHABETICAL LIST OF NAMED ENGINES

261

264

268

274

281

Notes

PRINTED FOR THE PUBLISHERS BY WILLIAM CLOWES AND SONS LTD
LONDON AND BECCLES
984.361

NOTES

NOTES

NOTES